WAKE AT WORK

WOKE AT WORK

Strategies to navigate the workplace and progress with pace

JOY OMOREGIE

Copyright © 2020 by Joy Omoregie

All rights reserved. No part of this publication may be reproduced, distributed, or transmitted in any form or by any means, including photocopying, recording, or other electronic or mechanical methods, without the prior written permission of the publisher or author, except in the case of brief quotations embodied in critical reviews and certain other non-commercial uses permitted by copyright law.

Woke at Work

A manual for thriving, not just surviving in the corporate world.

CONTENTS

Introduction - Why I wrote *Woke at Work* 1

PART ONE: HOW IT BEGINS 7

Chapter 1: My Journey into the Corporate World 8

Chapter 2: My Awakening 19

Chapter 3: Guide to Global Organisations 28

PART TWO: THE FUNDAMENTALS 37

Chapter 4: New Job! Start Strong and Stay Focused 38

Chapter 5: Attitude for Acceleration 48

Chapter 6: Prioritisation – Urgent vs Important 55

Chapter 7: Build Your Strengths and Develop Your Weaknesses 62

Chapter 8: Case Study – *Bossing It* 70

PART THREE: FRAMEWORK FOR SUCCESS 77

Chapter 9: New Team – Dynamics and Strategies 78

Chapter 10: Being Visible – Spotlight and Shine 86

Chapter 11: Mentors at Work 90

Chapter 12: Sponsors help you move – Watch out for motives 95

Chapter 13: Team Dynamics Part 2 – Competition and Progress 100

PART FOUR: MANAGING YOUR CAREER 105

Chapter 14: Career Planning – Best Practice 106

    Scorecards and Objectives 108

    Your career development plan 113

v

Chapter 15: Performance Review Meetings
– Best practice 118
Chapter 16: Internal Promotions and Job Moves 126
Chapter 17: Winning CV and Interview Prep 134

PART FIVE: THE DOs AND DON'Ts 143
Chapter 18: Meetings – Dos and Don'ts 144
Chapter 19: Emails – Dos and Don'ts 150
Chapter 20: Work Relationships – The Essentials 158
Chapter 21: Lost your Focus? Get it Back! 164
Chapter 22: Mistakes – Bouncing Back 169

PART SIX: TIME FOR CHANGE? 173
Chapter 23: Leaving Wisely 174
Chapter 24: Leadership – From Junior to Senior 181
Chapter 25: Becoming a Manager 188
Chapter 26: Managers – Supportive vs. Unsupportive 194
Chapter 27: HR – Cases and Strategies 201

PART SEVEN: THE NEW NORMAL, PRIVACY AND NETWORKS 211
Chapter 28: Being *Woke at Work* in a Virtual World 212
    Virtual professionalism 213
    Keeping up your engagement virtually 216
    Networking in a virtual world 217
    Career progression in a virtual world 218
Chapter 29: Trust and Privacy 221
Chapter 30: Professional and Social Networks 227

PART EIGHT: STAY TRUE TO YOU 235
Chapter 31: Remain Connected to Your Vision 236
Chapter 32: Beat Procrastination and Live with Purpose 244

Acknowledgements 250

INTRODUCTION

WHY I WROTE *WOKE AT WORK*

THIS BOOK BRINGS TOGETHER insights learnt over a decade within the corporate world. It contains so much of what I needed to know at various points along my career journey, but often discovered too late or learnt the hard way. When writing this book, my aim was to put key information in the hands of anyone aspiring to have a corporate career and also support the many talented individuals journeying through, trying to make upward progress. Many people journey through their careers, focusing on working hard and getting paid - simple. I certainly had that mindset for many years. But whilst hard work still pays off, I came to realise that many other important components are involved in driving progress within large organisations.

Entry points into the corporate environment can vary greatly. In addition to the skill and experience needed for the job, some people enter mentally prepared and guided about how large organisations operate. They start off with an idea of the key moves to make and the best way to conduct themselves in that environment to drive their progress. Others enter with their skills and experience but no frame of reference or insight into how things operate within the corporate environment. This often unknowingly puts them at a disadvantage from the start. They get burned early or just badly and exit without achieving their potential. Then there are those that start off somewhat prepared, only for struggle and stagnation to occur later down the line.

I came from a background that was very aspirational but nobody around me had worked in a large corporate environment at the time. I started my career full of energy and enthusiasm, focused on working hard and just going with the flow, enjoying the new experiences and novelty of working for such prestigious organisations, literally just sleepwalking through my career wearing rose tinted glasses. It took me years to understand vital aspects of career progression. I did not have an intentional focus on my progress, and I was oblivious about the workings of the workplace environment. It was years into my career journey, after experiencing some tough situations and a few negative cycles at work, that I began to wake up. There were key things I needed to know, attitudes to have, challenges to anticipate and face, things to be done and overcome.

In hindsight, I needed a manual or a guide on how to navigate and accelerate within this environment; a collection of that "know-how," those valuable things that I was not taught and could not draw from my network at the time. *Woke at Work* is that manual I wish I had had. It would have saved me a lot of wasted years without direction and helped me to avoid many mistakes. You do not have years to waste. The intention of the book is to accelerate progress and close the information gap surrounding how the corporate world works. Through the eight-part journey, across thirty-two chapters, I share tools and strategies that are vital for progress in the workplace whilst also keeping the focus on you, your life, your dreams, and your choices.

Having worked primarily within global banking and financial services institutions, in a variety of roles in the UK and Europe, with stints in Latin America and the Middle East, many of the examples I share relate to the dynamics within large global organisations, but the content and principles are transferable and can be applied to a variety of workplaces. At the start of the book, after some insight into my personal story and trigger moments, I take time to outline the typical large corporate organisational structure, particularly for the benefit of new entrants to the corporate world. I then present core fundamentals, the framework for success, career management and a plethora of strategies and approaches for a wide variety of aspects, in order to strengthen all readers.

For those at the start of your corporate career, the content of this book is invaluable. For those with more career experience, where principles are known, the refresher will help refocus your actions. There will also be many new ideas, perspective-shifting work, and life management approaches, as well as nuggets of wisdom that I hope will serve as new fuel to give you momentum at whatever stage you read this book.

During my corporate career journey, I was trained and accredited as a sales performance coach with a global consultancy, equipped to deliver highly effective coaching to underperforming sales teams. I worked with a range of managers one to one and each time, by injecting passion to see them unlock their potential and sharing key information and new strategies, I witnessed individuals shift their entire way of working. Whole teams moved from sluggish, comfort zones, to goal-focused individuals delivering amazing results. I have poured that same coaching energy, motivation and passion into this book.

Too many amazingly talented people fall into struggles at work and after a few bad experiences and badly knocked confidence, they stop fighting to reach their goals and true potential. *Woke at Work* empowers you to handle and overcome challenging situations, whilst also keeping your wellbeing and life goals in focus.

So now, let me explain the title.

As we all know, *woke* is a verb, an action, and the past tense of the adjective "to wake." Looking at the definitions of "to wake" really explains my intention behind this book. See below:

Wake – *emerge or cause to emerge from sleep.*

This is just so key for all of us when it comes to work.

Wake – *become alert to or aware of.*

Yes! Another critical key - You become more aware and alert to the reality of your working environment and this helps you ensure that as you put in the work, it also works for you.

Wake – *cause to stir or come to life.*

My hope is that you will be stirred and empowered to come to life at work, fully harnessing your strengths, talents, and the opportunities around you.

I want you to be *woke* – already awake and no longer sleeping when it comes to the workplace. Through reading this book, you will have access to key material that if followed, will help you become more aware of the workings of the corporate environment and hopefully help you take the right steps at the right time.

The title also harnesses the more recent use of the word *woke*; originating in African American vernacular English, meaning "to be alert to injustice" or "having greater social awareness." The workplace can be full of situations that seem unfair; occurrences that seem to favour the few; or actual examples of blatant discrimination. Being conscious of the variety of scenarios that can occur and developing the behaviours, mindset and actions required to overcome challenges and achieve positive outcomes, is my definition of being *woke at work*; managing yourself in the best possible way to stay in control of yourself, your career journey and your career progression.

If you are currently trying to navigate out of a challenging work situation; read! If you are not currently experiencing any challenges, then prepare yourself also by reading. Being *woke at work* is about increasing your ability to anticipate a variety of work situations and dynamics so you can position yourself to make optimal moves. If you have not yet entered the workplace or, more specifically, a corporate environment, you are fortunate to be reading this book now. Read intentionally and build a solid understanding of what to expect and a foundation for rapid progress.

Make a commitment to invest the time to read the book and apply the advice and guidance as often as you need it. It is your support manual to help you navigate the workplace and progress with pace. Regular review will help you stay "woke" and wise, and hopefully winning on your career journey.

PART ONE

HOW
IT
BEGINS

Remember key steps

CHAPTER 1

MY JOURNEY INTO THE CORPORATE WORLD

IT CERTAINLY HAS BEEN A CAREER JOURNEY, with many enjoyable aspects as well as tough challenges to overcome – internally and externally. However, there is something I want you to digest at whatever stage you are at right now in your career. If careers are journeys, then there should be a target destination, a vision for where you want to go and what you ultimately want to attain. Do not lose sight of this. This book will give you an insight into how to define your career path and remain focused in an ever-changing landscape. Concentrate and you will be empowered to jump the hurdles that often trip people up, and dodge the pitfalls that others experience. To achieve ultimate success within your career, one of the most valuable journeys to take is that of self-realisation and transformation. I will share now, how my journey began and the discoveries made very early on in my career.

I grew up in a humble working-class environment. My parents migrated in the early 1980's from Nigeria to the UK and worked consistently to provide for me and my three younger siblings. Our upbringing was full of love and security, strengthened through our Christian faith and family spirit. Both parents repeatedly told us that we could be anything we wanted - not even the sky was the limit. School was fun; the standard comprehensive system, big classes, noisy lessons and all students progressed through, whether they were good or bad. We had a structured curriculum and there were opportunities for everyone.

When asked that formative question during childhood, "What do you want to be when you grow up?", some said, "An ice cream van man." Others said, "an astronaut," some "a doctor," a few "a lollipop lady." I didn't know what to call my dream. I just had this image of being a grownup, in a suit, with a briefcase. A powerful looking woman. That was it. That was the vision. As we grew, some friends began to aspire to get pregnant to secure a "free flat" as their big sisters had, or very entrepreneurial guys turned to petty crime, frustrated with the delayed gratification of converting fifteen years of study into a regular job. I just had to hold onto my vision and remember that all things were possible if I could just believe.

School days really shaped my view of the workplace. From the initial belief that teachers cared about our progress, which many did. To treating others fairly and equally, and valuing teamwork over solo shining - no cheating, etc. "One day all this education will guarantee you a great job," they said. This was the life prep ingrained in my brain for fifteen years. In my mind, the workplace would simply be a more grownup version of school: you just work hard, bosses would then recognise your work and you would be promoted – simple.

After school, A-levels and college were concluded with last-minute bursts of revision, retakes and thankfully solid final results. This launched me into university life. I was the first in my immediate family to go to university and placed a huge amount of pressure on myself. Thoughts of all the young people who would be looking up to me as the first – coupled with all the adults who believed I was capable of so much, I just had to do well for them. My final term was stress! Pure stress but I graduated with a 2:1 in Economics and Development studies, which completely released the pressure I had stacked on my shoulders.

After a month or two celebrating the amazing post-university freedom, the reality of my student debt ended that party. As supportive as my parents were, repaying my student debt was down to me. I needed to get a job and I had graduated during a recession. Things felt very uncertain. That feeling of impending doom as headlines bombarded us, story after story with bad news, crises, economic meltdown, established companies and individuals gone with the wind. I can still recall that sense of chaos and uncertainty. Jobs were scarce, but my reality was: I needed to work. That student debt was looking at me, so I had to get out there and start looking for a job.

The year I graduated, the world was in the midst of a recession and graduate schemes had either tightened their entry requirements or completely cancelled their intake. Even with my 2:1 degree from Sussex University, and three years' experience working part-time for two global banks, I just could not get hired. My only option was to put out my CV as widely as possible. I want in hunt mode. I would get on the phone as soon as I saw vacancies with a contact number, and just applied for everything!

After so many rejections or not even getting a response, the one job that came through was a two-month temporary admin role. I was definitely overqualified but I just went for it. I turned up for the interview in a suit and heels, fully energised and determined to get the job. After a round of questions I had built some rapport and the conversation just flowed. That very day, just a few hours later, I was notified that I had secured the job. I was so happy and relieved. As they gave me further details, there was one major curveball - the actual role was on a construction site. No suit and heels required. It would be my job to sit in a cold warehouse, printing site access cards for builders. After all that study, my first job was sitting in a hi-vis jacket and tracksuits, making many interesting connections with construction workers from all over the world. I ended up being promoted into the site logistics team but after just two-months, the project completed and my temp contract ended. I was unemployed all over again and what I thought might be a few weeks, ended up being five months. I could not believe it.

Initially, I tried to stretch and manage the meagre savings I had accrued but after three months, the money had pretty much dried up. I had been actively seeking work but I was advised to sign on for Jobseekers Allowance so that I could prove that to potential employers and explain my employment gap. I had never experienced government support so I pushed back. As the unemployment continued I had no choice but to eventually start "signing on." That was hard for me.

As I reluctantly began the weekly visit to the Job Centre and the savings from the temp job eventually dried up, I really had to look at my life. Many of my post university dreams seemed completely out of sight. I was broke and feeling so disappointed. I had a real crossroad moment, two options – to give up and see my situation as one of lack and hopelessness or to look for the positives and become really conscious to the abundance I possessed. I took the second option. I became so thankful for life, health, family, friends, my home, food provided, my mind – full of hopes, dreams and ambition. I was so much more than my unemployed status. Even though I had no titles and no money, I realised I was so rich, so blessed and full of potential. It was time to hope, pray and act!

With renewed enthusiasm for life, I got on the phone and eagerly called up everyone online offering jobs. After many rejections and dead ends, I got through to a recruiter, gave my strongest opening pitch and we hit it off. I did not waste words; I shared the best of me and built rapport immediately. I was invited to an assessment centre which I passed and was then offered a job just a few weeks later. Such an amazing breakthrough.

The job was intense, lots of cold calling and high targets. I initially avoided breaks and sat glued to my desk trying to make up the numbers. One very sunny day, I took the rare decision to step out for a proper lunch break. I couldn't resist that great weather and enjoyed a long stroll in the city. To my surprise, I bumped into a family friend I had not seen since childhood. After trying to place how we knew each other, it hit us and we began to catch up. As we discussed, she mentioned where she worked. The name triggered my mind and I literally paused for a moment in shock. That morning I received a job advert for my dream job and from what I could remember, it was at the company she had just mentioned.

She was a manager there and after confirming that the role was live, she asked to see how I planned to present my CV. After her review, she very honestly said, "Joy, this would not have got you through the front door." From that point on, she focused on me presenting me. She focused on helping me to shift my CV from an outline of my previous jobs, to a two pager that showcased the great things I had personally done/achieved in each role. By the time I had restructured my CV and added my key achievements, I could not believe it. My CV was alive! It truly reflected ME. After that she spent weeks helping me to prepare for the interview process. Such an amazing help. She became my first mentor.

From thirty applicants, after five rounds of interview, I was one of the final two people. The hiring manager was visibly in a dilemma about which candidate to select. A week or two later I got the email and broke down in tears. I didn't get it. My temp job then abruptly ended a month later. Back to square one and those feelings of deflation, but I rooted deep into my faith and gained strength to persevere. I eventually got another temp job that, again, I was overqualified for. My work was easy, so I offered to help any other teams that needed support. In the process of helping, I was picking up a range of new skills.

One morning I received an email from a familiar name. It was the person who had interviewed me for the dream job. There was another job they were hiring for and she thought I would be suitable for this new role. The deadline had passed but she asked me to send my CV and cover letter if I was interested in applying. I couldn't believe it. As I read the job description it sounded like such a great role for me. I also had most of the required experience listed.

I got in touch with that mentor who worked at the company and she helped me pull together all my relevant experience. The additional tasks I had volunteered to do in the temp job, were actually some of the required skills requested on the job description for the new job. Everything was so divinely aligned. Within two months, I had landed an amazing entry-level job in a global multinational organisation in the middle of a global recession. All the experiences, and ups and downs throughout the year had been preparing me for this amazing new job.

It took eighteen months of postgraduate growth and support from unexpected people. I learnt the power of focus, persistence, recovering from setbacks, staying full of hope and always being ready to show up as my best self. My biggest strength came from my faith, which got me through the challenges and paved the way for new opportunities.

Hello, Canary Wharf! Shiny tall buildings, everyone in suits. The air even smelt like success. I could have just danced through the streets. My vision had come to life and I was now *her*: the woman with the briefcase. Well, in fifteen years the briefcase had evolved into a pretty, black tote bag. My childhood dreams had now become a reality and I was amazed. I had made it - the first person in my family to work in such a prestigious environment. I was so pumped with energy. Everything was possible and I was ready to change the world. The job fitted my personality, experience and passions so perfectly. It was a miracle! I was using my energy and creativity to bring goodness into the workplace and drive inclusive ways of working. Every day, my focus was on fair treatment of all employees, coaching managers on how to build diverse teams and overcome bias. I loved it. Within a year I had transformed an underdeveloped area into a recognised business function. Things were wonderful. I was just floating, giving love, and feeling loved by work.

I didn't have any perspective at the start of my career. I was just excited to be working in Canary Wharf. Amongst my friends, I had one of the best jobs. From unemployment to the top of the pile. I was so grateful. I floated on a 'Cloud Nine' corporate honeymoon for a few months. I felt like I was at the top, like I had made it. In reality, I was at the entry point and actually starting at the bottom. I began to realise I was in a whole new environment. Things operated so differently to what I had been used to. There was a new level I needed to operate at. I also began to realise something else. In several situations, I was the *only*: the *only* female, or the *only* black person, the *only* millennial, the *only* state school kid. Rather than having a negative impact on me, I felt like a trailblazer, paving the way for others. I celebrated being in the room. My plan was to just focus on working as hard as I could. That was my plan for success. In my experience that had always paid off but, as I would come to realise, I didn't know what I didn't know.

> **Wisdom nugget:**
>
> *Anytime you are the "only", see it as an opportunity to present whatever group you represent in the most positive light. How you conduct yourself and the fragrance you leave either helps to open or further close the door to others like you.*

As I began to attend external events as part of my role, I began to network, building connections with other people across my industry. These events gave me the opportunity to listen to their experiences, projects and discover what they were earning, too. As I began to benchmark myself, I soon realised I was achieving more than many of my peers but being paid much less. My 'Cloud Nine' bubble burst. What? I couldn't understand it. I was doing a great job, receiving great feedback, working above and beyond my job brief, so why didn't my manager just proactively increase my salary? Surely that should have been the obvious response to my effort? Questions just whizzing in my head. There was a new niggling feeling inside which could not be ignored but, the thought of discussing my salary gave me a worse feeling. How awkward and confrontational. What right did I have to bring up this issue with my manager? How would they receive such a conversation?

My mid-year review was coming up, so that seemed like the most sensible place to discuss this matter. I prepped as best as I could. I didn't want to rock the boat and wind up being unemployed again, but this was something that needed to be raised. Thoughts whizzed through my mind and I almost backed out of the conversation, but I knew it was justified. I decided to summon up the courage and go for it. I presented my findings of salaries for similar roles, highlighting all the successes I had driven for the company and politely presented my case for a pay increase, to bring it in line with the industry and reflect my contribution.

"You're right. What you have done has been brilliant, above and beyond your initial job description," my manager responded. I was shocked and elated. I was eager with anticipation for what would follow, as she continued, "But we didn't ask you to do all that." Mic drop. The elation deflated. I was then told that my job and salary would be staying the same, but to recognise all my hard work, they had decided to give me a token bonus of £250. I pasted a smile on my face and walked out of the room, confused and bewildered. I was in my early twenties and felt like some injustice had just happened, but I was powerless. I didn't have a professional network or anyone around me who had experienced this kind of situation, so I just remained puzzled. I was also so grateful to have a job that I didn't want to do anything further that could cause me to lose it.

In hindsight, I learnt a lot about what happened in that scenario. These were my first steps to waking up and they formed part of the events that linked together to open my eyes to opportunities arising in unexpected situations.

Wisdom nuggets:

- *Be prepared to step out bravely, despite how challenging the situation appears to be. Stay focused, keep connecting with people, making calls and applications. Go for it!*

- *No experience is wasted. In your period of waiting for your dream, don't waste the opportunity you have to gain new skills and experiences in odd jobs or even volunteering. Grow and become a better version of yourself for when your dream job arrives.*

- *If you don't value yourself, it is likely others won't value you either.*

- *Money should never be your sole motivation in your career but keep in mind the value you bring and ensure that your contributions are being valued accordingly.*

- *Always look on the bright side of life. Giving thanks can literally make you feel much better. Gratitude is humbling and shows appreciation in your lowest moments. Expressing gratitude can help you deal with adversity.*

CHAPTER 2

MY AWAKENING

THERE ARE MOMENTS that can occur in a person's life when they profoundly experience an awakening. Sometimes it can be sudden, like a lightbulb *Eureka* moment. Other times it can be a gradual waking up. If we drill down to the lowest level, we can see that awakening is itself a process that challenges our very core and ways of thinking. The framework which you operate on is reviewed, destabilised, and your perspective shifted.

The awakening that I will share now was the catalyst for me becoming *woke* at work and simultaneously experiencing a greater awareness about myself, the choices I had, and the need to wake up to how the world of work operated. By the end of this book, as you journey through chapters written to help you become *woke* at work, my hope is that you will gain a deep understanding of your reality in relation to work and life, and integrate new approaches to help strengthen you on your career journey. The wake up begins...

The mid-year review I previously spoke about was an interesting experience and my first real corporate wake-up moment. That appraisal outcome left me feeling dejected and made me feel like leaving. I had tried and failed to get a pay rise and felt that the organisation was willing to utilise me, my skills and what I was bringing to the table but keep me at a lower level than I was operating at. I had never had the desire to look externally for a new job but that would make sense. I just didn't have the same confidence. If they did not value all I had done in this company, how could I convince them of my value somewhere else? These are the types of questions I agonised over, day in and day out. This may well remind you of times you have felt something similar. Disappointment and rejection. What a combo. Very low moments that cause you to question your worth, power and ability to overcome.

Change can be difficult, but in general, should be viewed as a good thing. Why? Because it breaks with the old and inevitably leads to growth. Things began to change for me before that mid-year review even happened; I just didn't know it. Opportunity can arise in the most unexpected ways and you need to be open to that to avoid blocking what could be your breakthrough.

Early on in the role, I had received my first set of new business cards and was sent to represent that company at an external event. After the main event, the networking session began in a huge room of professionals. I felt like a tiny fish in a big pond. Looking around and hearing the buzz of so many conversations, posh laughter and seeing a room full of tailored suits and sharp outfits, my heart just started beating rapidly. I didn't even know where to start. I gave up on the networking idea and went straight to the delicious free food laid out in abundance. I collected my complimentary drink and canapés and sheepishly backed away into a corner. What on earth would I say? Nerves came over me. I even had to read my business card to remind myself of my official title!

I was just intending to eat enough canapés to count as dinner and leave, when I noticed another lady had backed into the same corner. We exchanged looks and it was like we were a mirror image of each other, the only difference being she was white, and I was black. Having things in common was enough for us to tentatively start a conversation. We found out we were both from London, we both knew about the London culture and working-class life and had both progressed from humble beginnings to work for a major corporate. It was an amazing connection. The two of us just hit it off, laughing about experiences, confessing how pretentious networking felt and just happy we could enjoy the rest of the event with someone who was real and down to earth. We swapped business cards, had last drinks, and went our separate ways.

A few months after the event, I was organising an event for senior women and looking through my collection of business cards to send invites to. I came across the card for that lady. As our conversation had flowed so naturally, it hadn't occurred to me to read her title or connect with her on LinkedIn. To my surprise, this super down-to-earth woman was a very senior professional. I eagerly sent her an invite, but her senior title made me feel like I had to be more professional, so I wrote a very formal message. She received it and replied in the same down-to-earth manner as before, saying she couldn't make my event but suggesting we connect for lunch at some point. That sounded great to me!

Our lunch catch-up was just like the networking event - great rapport and as we discovered more about our worlds of work, there were even more parallels in what we were both doing. We met for lunch roughly every six months after that, and each time I would share some of my recent successes and big goals. She often smiled, listening to everything I was doing and would offer nuggets of advice or perspective. One of our meetings happened to fall on the day of that mid-year review. I hadn't realised it was the same day, but an hour after feeling dejected and hopeless, my phone went off reminding me of this catch-up. I had to quickly refocus my mind and switch into my best self.

During our meeting, the experience of the mid-year review went to the back of my mind. As we got into a discussion, about halfway into the meeting, out of nowhere she asked if I wanted to remain in my current business area. Puzzled, I just shared that I had never planned to be in that area, it had just happened. She then landed a question that rocked me: "Would you consider leaving your organisation?" I was like "Excuse me?" As I looked at her, puzzled, she said that after hearing about my accomplishments over our catch-ups, she felt I would be a suitable candidate for a role she was hiring for. I couldn't believe what I was hearing. She had seen my talent and all I could feel was a sense of guilt fill my body. In that moment, I realised I felt such a deep sense of loyalty to my employer. They had given me my first real opportunity, so I felt like it was my duty to work for them. Rather than feeling excited about someone recognising my talent and telling me about a new opportunity, I just had a feeling of guilt and fear. Despite the figurative corporate hot-slap I had just received during my mid-year review, this conversation felt like I was betraying them.

Questions whizzed through my head. I didn't even think such conversations happened. I questioned whether I would even be qualified enough to go for a new job that, again, I had never heard of. My transferable skills, energy and experience had made her believe I was an ideal candidate, but it wasn't the standard process of applying for a job, going through an interview and meeting the manager at the final stage. This process was happening in reverse. As I had never been approached for an existing role, I felt I was doing something wrong, cheating somehow because I did not even know about the role and hadn't even applied for it. At the time I had no idea that many new jobs can start in this way. I was a suitable candidate for the role and was being headhunted by the hiring manager. I had no idea what headhunting was. I later found out it was a GREAT thing.

Rather than showing interest and going for it 100%, I dragged my feet with the lady. She patiently invited me for interviews with her team and other stakeholders. It went really well and within a month, I had been offered a new role and they were eager for me to accept. A networking event had opened the doors for me to work for another global corporate organisation. In addition to that, there was a serious salary increase too.

This was brilliant. Kick-started just an hour after that mid-year review but, can you believe it, the feelings of disloyalty and betrayal just amplified? I decided to mention the new opportunity to my existing employers. I thought it might make them review my mid-year outcome more positively and give me a reason to stay. They actually thought I was bluffing when I first presented it to them. When they realised I was being serious and it was a real opportunity, they offered me a few internal conversations to discuss what I was interested in doing in future, but that was it.

My final decisive moment came when the most senior manager I worked with, realising the job was a real prospect for me, arranged for us to have a meeting to discuss. I felt so honoured that she would take time out of her schedule to have a conversation about me. However, the whole conversation was geared towards talking me out of the new opportunity with no tangible incentive presented for me to stay. During the conversation, I got that internal nudge on the inside and knew I had to go with the new role. The very moment I shared that, the senior manager ended the meeting. It was so cold and final. I felt abandoned. But at that moment I realised, even though it is difficult, you have to follow your convictions and do what is right for you.

I exhaled the tension and accepted the role. The most amazing thing was that as soon as I made the decision, just like with the previous roles, things rapidly started to align around the new role. A contact who could give me insights on all I needed to know for the new role immediately entered my life and more, and I realised it was absolutely the right move.

In summary, even though I had loved my time there, I had to focus on my life, my goals and my opportunities. Much of my internal thinking needed to be rewired and when I eventually settled on the best decision for me, I took a leap of faith and stepped bravely into the unknown. What followed were new opportunities to grow, have greater impact and I received a much a bigger salary.

> **Wisdom nuggets:**
>
> - *Headhunting is a process of recruiting a prospective employee who is working elsewhere and who has relevant work experience for a particular job profile (HR Dictionary).*
>
> - *Even if you are happy with your current job, network with other people through events and maintain a professional profile on LinkedIn. Keep in touch with recruiters and maintain a good rapport so they remember you.*
>
> - *Don't feel like you have to hide your talents or strengths. Strive to be in environments that demand what you offer and encourage you to shine.*

Be careful not to form emotional attachments with your place of work because it can stop you from objectively managing yourself and pursuing your purpose.

Work isn't school. Managers are not like your teachers, so remove emotion and view work as a business relationship. You are in a place where you are there to add value, and to be valued and supported to develop. The workplace environment will gladly take from you but may not always reward you with new opportunities, so be aware of the options you have.

You don't automatically get recognised, progressed or get rewarded even if you are shining.

As you are working hard delivering and adding value in your work, you should be receiving commensurate value for your time and effort. Sometimes those that will value your talent and skill may be outside of your immediate team or business area.

When you start in your career in the corporate world, you may feel like the top amongst your friends or fellow students, but you are usually at the bottom of the workplace and have to work your way up.

Be open.

My major breakthrough started in the most seemingly random of ways. Make connections and be open to learn from others and share the great things you have done. It can lead to great opportunities.

I experienced many more wake-up moments: learning to deal with limiting beliefs, to overcome suboptimal approaches, wishing I had made different decisions after a situation passed, working out how colleagues, managers and teams functioned and how to work more optimally. The rest of the book is dedicated to sharing the key learnings I discovered. I have put these approaches together in practical ways to make them as accessible and transferable as possible.

As I look back, there was purpose in it because, having to discover this information the hard way is what has given me the content for this book. So, whether you are preparing to start your career, or you are already going through the journey of discovery, my hope is that this book will assist and guide you on the best approaches to progress. The next chapter will give an overview of global organisation, structures and roles. This understanding builds a crucial foundation for everything else. If you are already familiar with these structures or currently working for a large global organisation, you can move on to the next chapter.

CHAPTER 3

GUIDE TO GLOBAL ORGANISATIONS

IT IS SO IMPORTANT TO UNDERSTAND how the organisation that you are working for is structured. Grasping how it fits together even at a high level, completely differentiates you from someone who entered like I did at the start of my career. I believed I was at the top and felt that I had really made it to land such a job. What I came to realise however, was that I was at the entry level and starting from the bottom. There is usually an expected progression journey and the earlier you are aware of it, the quicker you can align to a development track and start your progression. In this chapter, I will be sharing an overview of global organisations and roles that you typically find in the corporate world.

The usual journey of progression in a global organisation is:

- Entry into country roles - based in, or serving, a specific country to gain experience at the market level.
- Strategic regional roles - based in or serving a particular region.
- Global headquarter roles that set the global strategy, usually located in the Headquarters (HQ) of the organisation but sometimes outside the HQ location.

This more "regular" path is seen as ideal because country roles enable you to gain front line experience. These are jobs that support the organisation's customers in that country directly. A company's customers or clients are the most important element. Without customers, there is no income. The products and services that any company produces, need to be bought for the company to survive, so the best companies focus on their customers. Understanding the customer needs, how the products can be improved, and how the customers can be best supported to use the products and services is of great importance to any organisation.

At the country or regional level, by directly working with clients or being closer to the customers' needs, you can better understand the products and services your company offers and the value that your organisation delivers to its customers. Core front line roles tend to fall within Sales, Product Management, Product Services, Customer Services, Marketing, Market Research and more. In global organisations, there are usually many junior entry-level customer contact roles – usually at a support or analyst level.

You will also have clients and vendors. A client is an alternative word for a customer. The term is used more to elevate the customer relationship. Describing the customer in this way makes the relationship sound more valued and personalised. In some roles, all customers are referred to as clients; in some cases, it is interchangeable; and in some cases, the term *customer* is in widespread use.

Vendors are companies that provide products or services for your organisation. In some job roles, your company will be hiring a vendor to add a product or service to something your company is trying to build or create. Any company being paid to offer a product or service to your company or team is your vendor. There will be a number of formal agreements that will need to be in place and signed before your business or team are able to work with them.

Many people start their career journey at the country or regional level. The reason for this is, by starting in country roles you bring your insight from the country/market level on the ground, into more strategic roles with a wider influence on the Regional or Global direction or the business area you work in. The rationale for this journey of progression is that when you start at the country level, you build more knowledge of the issues on the ground and feed them up into the company strategy.

Sometimes however, it happens that people start off going straight into the global head office of a large global organisation, just as I did. In that case, the expectation is that you have some form of strategic insight that you can bring, as you are expected to be supporting teams that have a strategic, multi region or global focus. Global roles are usually further removed from the selling and customer-facing activity, and more focused on setting the direction and governance for how the regions and countries will operate.

Now particularly for those starting out in your career journey, I will use the analogy of a car to create a picture of the components of a large corporate organisation. The business and company will have core functions: Business Management, Operations, Strategy and Governance, Audit, Compliance, Legal, Finance and Human Resource management. These would make up the corporate engine, which has the most components involved in making sure that the car functions. Most roles in the corporate world fall into this space – critical for it to keep moving. The car also needs to look good (Design, Research and Development). It needs quality features and build (Product Development, IT Infrastructure). It also needs to feel good (Customer Experience) and have a response unit for any issues with the car (Customer Services). Finally, for getting the car to marketplaces (Sales, Marketing, Communications, etc.).

Being in a large organisation can be viewed from two perspectives: daunting and overwhelming, or full of opportunities to grow in many directions. Take the latter view! It gives you access to many business areas and possible opportunities. Having a global network of offices, opens up the option of working abroad within the company. By communicating my interest in other countries to my managers, saying "yes" to new projects and connecting with my colleagues located in countries of interest to me, I have been able to work in the Middle East, Latin America and Europe, in addition to role based in the UK. Many things are possible.

When you start working within a global or large organisation, turn any fear you may have into curiosity and be bold! Maximise what it offers you: the countries, variety of roles, so many different areas and possibilities. There are lots of opportunities to work in many locations and business functions, but it is also very important to understand how the organisation works. Most organisations are usually shaped in a pyramid in terms of jobs. The base having most of the jobs; roles that are simpler, following a repeated set of processes but usually requiring many individuals to churn out high volume work. As the job levels get higher, the roles become more senior, involving more complexity, management, and leadership responsibility.

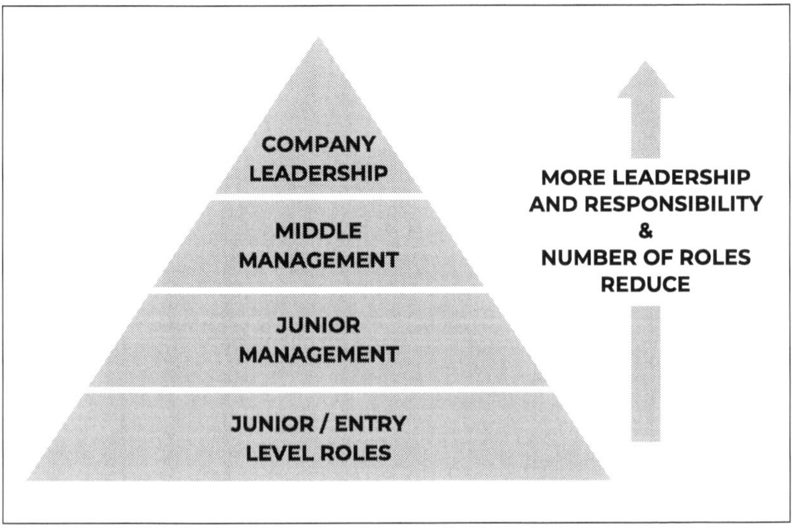
COMPANY LEADERSHIP
MIDDLE MANAGEMENT
JUNIOR MANAGEMENT
JUNIOR / ENTRY LEVEL ROLES
MORE LEADERSHIP AND RESPONSIBILITY
&
NUMBER OF ROLES REDUCE

The number of roles at higher levels reduce until you arrive at the top of the pyramid where the Managing Directors, CEO, President, Chairperson, etc. reside. As I was clueless about this at the start of my career, I would suggest that you research how the career progression levels work before joining a company, or early on after joining. This gives you a better perspective and awareness into how the organisation is structured and where you fit in that whole structure.

A lot of this information is available online on job sites, and even on YouTube for some of the biggest organisations, so use them to get prepared. HR is the function within an organisation responsible for all aspects related to the employees: this includes functions like recruitment and hiring, onboarding new joiners, giving manager guidelines, creating frameworks for employee welfare, facilitating job moves, governing performance management systems and conducting employee grievance or disciplinary procedures. We will look more into the latter within Chapter 27: HR cases and strategies.

When you enter a new organisation, check for information on job bands or grading. These are the levels of progression in your organisation. There should be information available on the central employee intranet that can provide you with a general overview of the levels, descriptions, and progression journey. For more in-depth understanding, you can organise a catch-up with your local HR person, or a senior manager who has been in the organisation for a while who you can connect with as a mentor. What you should be asking is how the company banding and grading structure works, along with a rough estimate of the types of salaries at each level, so you get a stronger sense of what the progression path looks like. View organisational charts for your area to understand the job roles, structures and progression levels in your area and company more broadly.

In an organisation, as roles become more senior, they will contain more elements of complexity and specialism, involving further responsibility for people or geographies, managing more risks, higher budgets, responsible for making tougher decisions, being given tougher targets to hit and usually additional pressure and accountability to more managers. Whatever job you are in is, therefore, an opportunity to build more knowledge, skill and experience which together prepare you to take on the responsibilities of more senior positions in the future. The main attraction for senior positions is often the increase in salary. This is a natural and expected motivation for new roles.

Environments can differ greatly. Observe and familiarise yourself with what professionalism looks like in that team and organisation. Make sure you understand your managers' expectations. This is just about understanding the immediate environment you are surrounded by so you can adapt accordingly. Adaptation is not losing yourself or becoming another person. It's you being able to present yourself in the best way for that professional environment. Like wearing a formal outfit for a wedding, a football kit for a match, casual clothes for a stroll or dressing up to go out with friends. In these four situations, you would be the same person – just different outfits and ways of operating in each environment.

The same goes for adapting to the organisation you are in. Aim to present yourself optimally for your environment and concentrate on effectively moving through the organisation, making the most of your time there. As an example, I usually wore my hair in slim straight braids for ease and style. One day I had a complete change; I arrived in a beautiful, tailored work dress, a sharp blazer and for my glorious afro hair I had chosen a hairstyle for work which was neat and clipped to the side, and just rocked it! I loved it. Colleagues also loved the new look. I was my authentic professional self. You don't have to be somebody else. Just be your best professional self.

As we move from the foundational understanding of the organisation you are in and your immediate environment, the insights and strategies that I will be sharing will really focus on strengthening you to anticipate situations that occur in the workplace and incorporate actions to boost your career progression. At this stage, we will move into laying the strongest foundations when you are starting a new job.

PART TWO

THE FUNDAMENTALS

Critical building blocks

CHAPTER 4

NEW JOB! START STRONG AND STAY FOCUSED

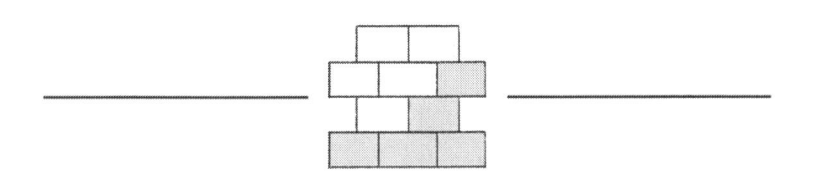

IT'S VERY NORMAL TO HAVE A SENSE of anxious excitement before you start a role. You're stepping into a new situation, meeting new people, and you also want to be able to do a good job. Depending on the type of person you are, there can also be nervousness too (which is very natural), driven by all the unknowns and your internal thought processing. Whatever your thoughts are, just keep in mind that you have been chosen, selected from a batch of candidates, and capabilities have been identified in you to support the business to grow. You have skills and experiences that are valuable for the new role and you need to put them into action.

Also remember, you are starting at ground zero again. Regardless of how skilled you are and the experience you have had, you will need to learn to understand and effectively function in your new role and new area.

Sometimes that feeling of being overwhelmed can start bubbling up. Nope! Don't allow it to take hold. You've got this. There's a reason you were hired for the job! You have what it takes so you have to kick negative thoughts and feelings to the side. Don't let them steal your power. The next five points are great to refer to, when you enter a new work situation. They help you keep your perspective and stay grounded:

- Understand yourself – What level are you at? What are your gaps? What do you need to learn? What can you confidently do currently – What are your strengths and core skills?

- Understand your environment – Who are the leaders? Who are those who can help you? Who are the ones that could be in competition with you?

- Be clear on where you are going – Do you like this area? Do you want to stay? Are you using this job as a steppingstone to take you further?

- Maximise opportunity – Find out what is coming up in terms of new work that gives you a chance to learn more and develop your skills. Take on work that gets you noticed by managers - Be visible!

- Build a strong network – Genuine relationships that will help you progress, learn or both.

These points are critical foundations every time you start a new role. In further chapters, we will explore each point in more detail and look at how you can practically implement them. The next section will be looking at the first day in a job. As you are reading this, even if you are currently in a role, use it to refocus your approach and your level of intention right where you are. Check against the points and put the framework for success in place as far as you need it.

FIRST DAY IN THE JOB

Onboarding – this is the term that is used to describe the process of joining a new organisation and Day One is crucial. You can never re-make a first impression. Attitude and approach are everything - humility really is my best recommendation. Be humble, my friend, be humble. It's a new situation and you need to ease in well. Confidence and being ready for action are great; that is the right attitude, but just be mindful to make sure you stay as far from arrogance as you can. Even if you have an amazing CV or your new hiring manager is singing your praises, be neither prideful nor over-eager like a new puppy. Instead, aim to be *you* on your best day; be polite, calm, and attentive to what you are hearing. Think more like a guide dog in training. The right attitude is having a readiness to learn, with a focus on ways to start adding value to your new team and manager as soon as possible.

Don't see your work as just a job. People often say that, but when you take that viewpoint it can affect your level of energy and engagement, which can make you approach each day looking forward to it being 5 pm (time to get out of there or log off) rather than looking at how you make that day count. I would say instead, see whatever job you are in as a moment in your life and an opportunity to build. See yourself as being there for a reason, for your benefit as well as the for the benefit of the Business. See your role as one with a purpose: to add value, demonstrate what you can do, create a positive impact, and develop as much as possible whilst you are there. Consistently maintaining this perspective will keep you in development mode, which will ultimately make you a stronger candidate for other jobs in the future.

Now in terms of first introductions to your team - on a first day, this can vary widely. I'll present a few scenarios:

1. **Low engagement** - You may start a role and your manager may not actually be there. A colleague comes to collect you, or you arrive and are just directed to where your team is. You could start in a virtual team situation where your first contact with your new manager and team is via a virtual meeting, being introduced via email. In all cases, your best action is to do what you can do to proactively form connections.

Introduce yourself, your new role and communicate that you are looking forward to working with and connecting with the team to understand more about them and their roles.

2. **Medium engagement** - your manager will introduce you as a new person and will often say something positive about you to position who you are, and your role within your new team and colleagues. That's normal and helpful - if it does happen, listen carefully to what is said about you in the introduction. Take

a mental note so you know of the first thoughts about your role. Communicate that you are looking forward to working with the team and connecting with everyone to understand more about them and their roles.

3. **High engagement** – your manager may have already billed you as the best thing since sliced bread. This is good but can also make you feel under pressure to be great before you have even said "hello." Don't fear this – they are talking about you, so just take a deep breath and step into it! Commit to making sure you deliver. Humbly communicate that you are looking forward to working with the team and connecting with everyone to understand more about them and their roles.

LEARNING MODE

Whether the new job is a move upward – promotion, or a lateral move sideways – different role at the same level, always remember that whenever a new role commences, you will be starting from the bottom. You have skills you will be bringing into the role and value to contribute but in this ever-changing world and the modern workplace, you cannot rely solely on a set of skills. Learn, Learn, Learn! My encouragement to you is: *always be ready to learn, adapt and grow.* Approach every new role, project and situation knowing that you will initially have to be in learning mode. The pace of change and development across people, processes and ways of working is rapidly changing; you can only keep up by staying in learning mode.

Create a learning plan to quickly start understanding core areas of your business. In the first week, I would strongly suggest you do the following:

- Ask your manager and team for all the key reading materials.

- Complete the mandatory training as soon as possible – usually on health and safety, conduct, behaviours, compliance, and organisational processes.

- Ask what the key priorities are for the business area; find out how your role fits into your team and the wider business area.

- Organise catch-up or introduction meetings with your core team members at a time that suits them. Aim to find out what they do, how they connect with your world of work and how you will be working together.

- Always aim to deliver tasks with quality and deliver ahead of time.

- Create a plan for the first month including the earlier priorities for you to deliver.

In addition to these points, obtain the organisational chart for your business. If your team does not have one already written, you can look it up online via your HR system. Use it to view your manager's managers – they will be the people who influence your area – it's important to keep them in mind and try and get an opportunity to introduce yourself to them. Get familiar with those at the same level as your manager - these other

43

managers will have teams that work with your area. Keep them in mind and introduce yourself as well, and when you start having interactions with them or their team members. Look at your manager's direct reports. This is your core team with whom you will be working most closely.

Take note of this information so you know exactly what you need to be doing from Day one. No more wasting precious time being directionless and looking for people to tell you what you have just read in this chapter. You have what you need. A solid framework to build on anytime you enter a new role. You just have to say to yourself; I am going to focus, be organised and cover all bases.

PROTECTING YOUR PERSONAL BRAND

Now from Day One, you will be communicating yourself to your new environment. The way you come across and how you are experienced by your colleagues within your workplace all relate to your personal brand. The way you conduct yourself and the work you do either advertises or hinders you. It is important to manage these aspects well from the start to the finish of your day, and throughout your career. When speaking about your personal brand, it is about your image and your reputation.

We all have different personalities, specific talents, strengths, and weaknesses/development areas. When you are in the workplace, it is critical to protect your reputation. As a starting point, I truly encourage you to always operate with integrity – which simply means to do what you know in your heart and conscience is the right thing to do – even when it is hard. Don't be led to believe that anything else is acceptable. Keep your conscience clear. Keep pushing forward in your role and be honest.

Your personal brand is how you are viewed by colleagues and is what you put out into your working environment. As far as possible, be your authentic self. The true you. Your best self. Of course, that means maintaining your professional manner in the process. We will touch on brand further into the book but here are a few initial tips that really help to protect your brand and your value:

- Don't gossip.

- Don't get involved in office negativity, or politics (tensions, negativity and unprofessionalism between people and teams).

- Learn what you need to know for your job. Focus on that first. You are not expected to know everything immediately.

- Do what you are hired to do – WELL. Follow instructions provided to get the job done accurately.

- If you discover more efficient ways of working, let your manager know and see where you can implement your new ideas

- Don't struggle in the wrong role for you. If you are in a role for a while (12-18months) and after much trying you are still not developing, look for a role that interests you or better suits your skills and personality and make a move

- Always utilise your strengths and be open to learning more and more as you progress.
- Understand what you do better than others. Make sure you showcase that and are recognised for it.
- Don't over commit and gain a reputation for not delivering on time or lacking quality.
- Don't hide your strengths or downplay them. Find a place that appreciates them.
- Maintain strong relationships at multiple management levels.
- Be genuine. Act with integrity.
- Be positive.

There are so many more elements related to how you protect your personal brand and I have highlighted them where relevant throughout the book. One other thing that really stands out is posture and presence. Standing tall, shoulders back, rather than slouching does so much for the way you come across. It communicates being more open and confident in yourself. I have also observed that having a more controlled glide in your walk, rather than just rushing around makes a difference and is noticeable. I saw the head of our business doing it - not a tall lady, but this was her style and it really made her come across more confidently and appear taller.

Finally, how you engage with your work environment is critical. The actions you take on your job - with your colleagues and managers, as well as with other teams, seniors, or your wider contacts outside the organisation – all affect the 3 P's: Progress, Pay Rises and Promotion. As important as they are, there is often a struggle to obtain them. It is important to understand your personality type, as it's the channel that you communicate through. If you are usually quite introverted or shy, keep in mind that you will not be able to function as an island and hope to secretly be discovered.

In the opposite way, if you're more extroverted and confident, be careful not to be perceived as being arrogant, loud or a busy body. Whatever your natural disposition, you want to get noticed for the right reasons. As the working world has rapidly shifted to more virtual working since the 2020 global pandemic, workplace engagement will inevitably be more digital, but there will still be an optimal way to engage. There is a whole section on this towards the end of the book called *Being Woke in a Virtual World*, so we will cover virtual engagement and professionalism in more detail there.

From optimum mind-set for your first day to setting your initial goals and priorities, the next chapter is about giving you insights into how to embed yourself into a new environment and build a foundation for acceleration.

CHAPTER 5

ATTITUDE FOR ACCELERATION

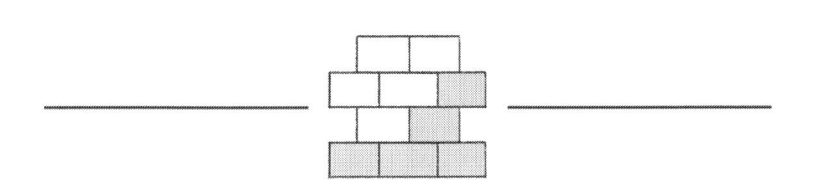

MORE THAN ANYTHING, your attitude and the actions you take are the deciding factors for your success. This will not be a motivational pep talk; it will highlight the reality of the attitude and actions required for you to accelerate and progress in your role, and the organisation you are in. It all depends on you deciding to take hold of this information and intentionally applying it to your life. Good results usually then follow that effort. Let's explore in more detail.

A good starting point for acceleration in your role is having a target for how long you want to spend there. Generally, two to three years is a usual length of time to be in a role before moving onto something else. It could be more or less. Anything more could signal that your role is evolving, giving you new skills and opportunities, or it could signal that you're getting comfortable and could be ready for a move. Less time in a indicates rapid acceleration or possibly that the role was not a good fit. In that optimal two-to-three-year period, your goal should be to transform from the level of knowledge you had at the beginning and aim to develop that to a greater level of knowledge and experience by the end. As you develop new skills, you take them from one experience or job to another. These transferable skills are great, but as new jobs/opportunities get harder these transferable skills can be heavily relied on as a crutch. Remember you will have to bite the bullet and learn new information or new ways of working. Use your core skills to help you, and focus on getting to the other side of that learning challenge. Imagine how much stronger it will make you!

The biggest barrier to you attaining that higher level of development is a willingness to learn new things. In a new role, the company will have training, courses and colleagues who can point you in the direction or show you how things work. Take the help and follow the approach of curiosity and discovery, commit to learning, apply yourself and master it. If there is anything you don't understand, get clarity on it. Ask around for things to be explained or ask to be given an overview then build on it through further reading and conversations. Demonstrate to your managers that you are actively learning as you discover what you need to know from connecting with colleagues and asking questions.

Get focus and direction by asking your manager or a trusted colleague to tell you what you need to know. This will save you from trying to wade through all the information on your own. The reality is that you will still need to read outside of the day-to-day work that you do. You will need to understand what has been done before and understand the wider context of the work that you are doing now. Learn to read around your business area and relevant topics. Set up Google alerts to pick up key pieces of information relevant to your area.

If you don't like reading or have a condition like dyslexia or a speed of processing condition, fear not: we all have different ways of learning; watching corporate videos, listening to audiobooks, taking video-based courses is the way to go. Just be intentional and master the topic. If you're a Project Manager, master the set of tools and processes that make amazing PM's. If you are in Sales – master client research, understanding customer needs, pitching structures, negotiation and hook. If you're in Strategy, master stakeholder management, understanding business needs, construction of business cases, and communicating business value.

Now in terms of your work ethic, always work to get ahead of time. Arrive early and finish things earlier than you planned. Give yourself time to review for errors as that will affect the view of your work and your brand. Also, remember that amazing work delivered after a deadline is similar to mediocre work delivered on time, as the amazing work does not exist when needed, and the mediocre work is there when needed but just not great. Deliver quality work on time or early. Let that become a habit. Be realistic about when you can do something and whatever you have promised, commit to it. Set a target and smash it! This is the definition of living your best life and maximising time.

The easiest yet most destructive action people take is wasting time. Time = Life. Wasting your time = wasting your life. Wasting time is costly and will affect your progress more than anything else. Value time. Respect it. Use it wisely. Manage it well. Maximise it. Beware of leaving tasks to the last minute, especially those with high visibility, audit, and regulatory requirements. These are high priority and if not done completely, they can expose you, your managers, and your team.

Many people coast along in their jobs, doing just what they need to get by. Just be aware of this, keeping in mind your own goal and work productively and at pace. Identify problems that you can see solutions for and suggest a better approach or method. You are not everybody else. You are you, on your own journey. Your journey is what you make it. In all your work, just try and complete it as soon as possible. Focus on your own journey. You have your own life to live; decide on your goals and ensure that you create the associated actions to hit them.

Independent study makes a massive difference and, when you apply what you have learnt to support your role, it also enables you to contribute more to the growth and performance of the team. Try and set aside a specific time that works for you - when you feel alert. Be practical about when it makes sense to get your reading done. In the early stages of your role, (first two weeks) it is highly acceptable for you to spend time reading and doing your training within your working day. There will be some mandatory learning that you will need to complete as a requirement for your role. Just get it done as soon as possible. For wider learning, be practical about making time for that – perhaps before work, the commute, breakfast hour, a lunch break, in the evening at home or just before bedtime: set a time limit to complete work and then go for it!

Your organisation is responsible for making sure you have what you need to do the job. If you need equipment for your job, ask for it. You are entitled to it. By having what you need to get the job done more efficiently, you are in a better position to add more value to the organisation, so they are investing in you. This is how you should think about new equipment or training your company pays for. Don't be afraid to make a request, just be reasonable about costs. Check if there are internal solutions before you look for external solutions. Have in mind – Why do you need it? What benefit will it bring to your work, team or company?

If it's an external qualification that will benefit your job and make you more productive, your organisation should be paying for it, too, as they will receive the benefit. In some organisations, if they pay, they may ask for two to three years' commitment in return before you leave the company. And if you do leave earlier because you have become a more attractive candidate with the qualification, then you may have to pay it back. This may not always be the case, but it does happen.

Key points to remember for acceleration:

- Your existing strengths and talents are the foundation to build on in a new job. Commit to learning new skills.

- Get into the habit of focus. It is the key to finishing tasks. Distractions are increasing and real focus can be very difficult. If you struggle with this, set times when you lock yourself away and leave personal devices in another room to concentrate on what you need to do.

- Fight the urge to constantly check your phone. If it isn't business-critical, ignore your personal phone until you have finished what you need to do. Lock it away. It will distract you and eat up valuable time and concentration. This will affect the quality of your output and you can't afford to let that happen for something you can enjoy later.

- Stay close to the manager's personal assistants (PA's) or executive assistants (EA's). They are such key team members. They often have useful information on what's going on because of how closely they work with the senior managers. If you have a good relationship, they can give you a heads up on key things coming up, or times when managers are available.

- Push mindset: How can you make your work even more valuable? Keep in mind that your role is to support your manager to achieve what they need to do by doing a great job on what you need to do. Before starting anything, at the point of instruction - clarify what is required of you and think about the task more broadly. What is it for? Who is it ultimately for? Who is the wider audience? What can you do to enhance it?

Wisdom nugget:

Work like you're on a mission! Push past that sluggish slowdown that creeps in just before you hit the finish line. Race hard and win!

The approaches I have shared above will cause you to stand out if you are consistent with them. Being consistent is what gets you recognised as someone who is adding value, finishing tasks and rapidly developing their depth of knowledge within the team and business area. This attitude is impressive to managers as it positions you as someone who is reliable for delivering on task and identifies you as a high potential candidate. Now from attitude, we are moving into some practical methods for how you manage your priorities and set your goals. Many things will come into your world whilst at work and you need to filter them and focus to make sure you are working on what matters most. This requires prioritisation, effectively managing your time and the expectations of your managers and colleagues.

CHAPTER 6

PRIORITISATION – URGENT VS IMPORTANT

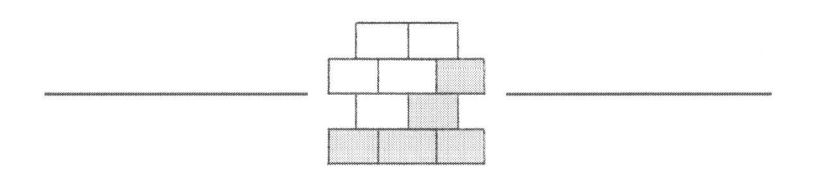

WORK CAN GET REALLY BUSY. That is normal. So many moments when actions and tasks are coming in thick and fast. Phone calls, emails, colleagues asking for things, training to be completed, meetings, etc. Just so much going on. I am not the best juggler and dropping balls is never a good idea! That dreaded moment when your manager has to chase you for a piece of work that you've let slip, or when you are working on too many things at the same time and stop making any progress. The best advice I can give on this is to be firm on what your priorities are and get rid of distractions so you can focus. Your manager's priorities should be on your radar and your priorities should align to support theirs. Understand from your manager the overall goals they have and what is required from you to help them achieve those goals, in addition to your work. Review your priorities with them and make sure you are on the same page about what you should be focusing on. Find out the strategic priorities or goals for your business.

How do you prioritise:

- You will have your set job; aim for it to be completed to a high standard and efficiently.

- Whatever your boss asks you to do becomes a priority. Find out when it needs to be ready and then organise a time to complete it as soon as possible and to a high standard.

- In a list of tasks, find out which ones are of most significance to the business – collaborate.

- Some tasks are not as important but become urgent – collaborate or delegate.

- Low-value tasks that build relationships – do them selectively but not consistently.

- Maintain your value. Don't get sucked into helping by doing all the admin. It can be a trap.

- Low value tasks that you work on alone, complete as quickly as possible and avoid in the future.

- Tasks that are quick to do, just clear them off your plate.

If your manager asks you to do something, see it as an opportunity to add to your brand. Look at how you can deliver the best result as quickly as possible. If you are told to prepare something and have time, don't waste it, get ahead of time. Prepare. With the extra time you have; are there ways you can enhance what is being asked of you?

The Eisenhower matrix was developed by President Dwight Eisenhower himself as a strategy to help him prioritize and deal with the many critical issues when he was leading the US Army and NATO forces, and eventually as president of the United States. He created what seems so simple; a quadrant assessing what was urgent and important. This concept when grasped is brilliant for organising your priorities. Things can just land in your life unexpectedly, and this system enables you to maintain control over your time, choices and helps you to stay focused on doing what matters. The focus is on what is *urgent and important* to you and your job. When you look at each new request through this lens, you can take the appropriate actions. Below I have expanded the urgent/important framework to bring it to life with four zones and their descriptions:

Eisenhower Matrix – Urgent and Important Analysis

	URGENT	NOT URGENT
IMPORTANT	**DANGER ZONE** Everything in this space has to become your priority. These tasks are all urgent and critical. They create stress or unease until they are complete. Finish them asap!	**GOOD ZONE** – These things matter to you, so they represent the most valuable use of your time. Create time for them and guard that time as other things in the urgent or not important zone will complete for your time.
NOT IMPORTANT	**AVOID ZONE** – These things are other people's priorities. Someone else's poor planning, desire for your help or attention. If you have time help/respond, if not – delegate.	**BAD ZONE** – stop doing these things. They are time stealers! Things you do that add no value to your life and rob the time you could be using for all the important things you need to do. This zone contains distractions.

The area that you have the least control over is *Urgent and Important – the DANGER ZONE*. Tasks in this zone must become your top priorities. They are important to you and have become urgent. Things like: your manager sets you a deadline and it is coming up, an application deadline, you have left mandatory training to the last minute, an important senior meeting just added to your calendar for the next day and you have to prepare work for it. Things here are all urgent and all-important to you. Tasks and actions that need to happen now. Priorities that fall into this box need to happen immediately. This box = rushing, stress, panic. Possible errors and mistakes could deliver a lower quality because of less time to properly prepare and approach calmly. Aim to resolve such tasks as soon as possible.

The *Not Urgent but Important – GOOD ZONE* – these are the things you should make time for. They will be of benefit to you if done, but you have to make time to do them. This is the most important box for your life. This is the planning and strengthening zone. As they are very important but not urgent, they often get pushed back. "I'll do this later." Things such as going to the gym, studying, research, prayer, rest, spending time with loved ones, planning ahead for your day, updating your CV, improving your analysis skills, finishing a book, etc.

The *Not Important but Urgent – AVOID ZONE* – things that fall in this area need to be delegated, rescheduled, or declined. These things are not important to you and only urgent because someone else interrupts your life, wanting you to participate urgently. Examples are a phone call, responding to notifications, last-minute requests for urgent assistance, helping someone else meet their deadline. These can rob you of your free time and land you in the urgent-important zone for things that are not important to you. They also rob you of valuable time that could be used for important but not urgent things.

Not Urgent and Not Important - BAD ZONE – stop doing these things. This is the WORST of all zones because it adds no benefit to your life. These include - excessive watching of TV, regularly oversleeping, procrastination, hours of shopping without actual need, excessive social media consumption. All rob time from your life and reduce the time you have left for what is important to you.

Organisation is critical when it comes to managing your priorities. Develop a simple routine or personal system that works for you; then be consistent. Just follow it every day. List at the end of the day what needs to be done tomorrow. Check the meetings coming up the next day, too. Then, start the new day checking that list, adding anything new to it and aim to cross it all off before the end of the day. Invest time in understanding the workflow for your job. What are the things you need to do on a daily, weekly, monthly basis? Put these into your diary. One of these should be your weekly priorities catch-up with your boss.

Categorise what you need to do as core areas/topics, then write the main goals in focus for you for that month – this then becomes a good list to check with your manager every week so you stay focused on the priorities and can discuss progress and stretch targets (additional things you can do to add more value to each of the goals or other pieces of work). Each week write out the smaller tasks you need to do to smash those goals/priorities.

Overcoming distractions:

Distractions come from everywhere. If you are in a "firefighting" team, where everything is always urgent **and** important, new things can land from nowhere and you can easily lose your focus. In such an environment, things that are urgent and important to you, have to be done immediately. This can involve needing to drop other less urgent and important tasks, in order to get the new items done. In other cases, where that urgent and important surprise task is not directly your responsibility, you may have the desire to help out but really assess if you have the extra capacity (time and energy) to do so.

It is great to support your wider team, but it's all about the time you have available and how you use it. Be careful about your focus becoming divided and diverted from what you actually need to be delivering personally. Helping out or working on other tasks should never be at the expense of focusing on your core list of priorities. Always aim to be the person that can be trusted to finish what you are asked to do, when you are asked to do it. Not the person with a list of a half started, unfinished, overdue list of tasks. Be your most efficient self. Finish your set tasks, then offer any remaining capacity within your working day, to helping out where needed.

I know of a super organised and efficient personal assistant (PA) who doesn't let a thing slip and controls the office to the finest detail. Now ask her about her personal life and that is where you will find mess and disorder. I say this because you may need to just focus on operating in your most structured and focused way for those 8-10 hours of work, even if your personal life has more catching up to do. Don't jeopardise your source of income or progress because of laziness and a chaotic way of working.

This Eisenhower matrix is a wonderful tool for just checking where a task fits so you can effectively prioritise it. We are now going to look at how you deal with the areas you feel weak in. Challenges you need to overcome. Nothing is impossible, but some things feel easier or more natural to do than others. These areas of development require you to face things that you dislike or struggle with, so they don't hinder you from developing and flourishing in your strengths. We will tackle how you build up your strengths and develop your weaker areas in the next chapter.

CHAPTER 7

BUILD YOUR STRENGTHS AND DEVELOP YOUR WEAKNESSES

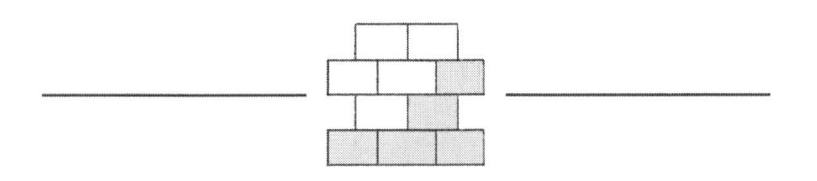

VERY EARLY ON IN MY CAREER, I asked one of my managers for the best advice they could give me. Their response was, "Find out early what you are good at and then get really good at it." I thought that meant just doing what I loved doing, but it really meant developing those skills. Move them from good to great. Make them sharper so that you can use them to really enhance aspects of your work that they are most relevant to you. As you progress, your job roles will take on additional parts that you may not be as strong in. You also may not like the new areas as much. These things still need to get done. They just become areas that you need to develop. This reality is so important to hold on to. It is rare to love every single aspect of your job but, you should aim to enjoy a lot of it. Then there will be other things that are involved in getting the job done that you will not enjoy but you will just have to face and conquer.

It is natural to want to run away from things you don't feel good at and don't like. I certainly did. As far as possible, I tried to make my job focus on what I was good at and where I could shine. There was some limitation in that approach and in reality, at the start of your career, your focus should be on building a well-rounded foundation of skills. That is why most large organisations create rotational graduate programmes to give new entrants broad experiences in various roles, to build a general set of skills required for business. Core skills like communication, stakeholder management, project management, data analysis, risk management, reporting and presentations, etc. Ideally, you should build on this foundation, developing more specialist skills and finding roles that play more to your strengths.

The corporate environment presents a lot of opportunities. Try and locate them and then target an opportunity to join a team doing work you enjoy. Some people enjoy the big picture – strategic projects, dynamic environments, working with a wide group of stakeholders, identifying what needs to be done for impact, setting direction and plans for delivery, etc. Others prefer structured environments, with set processes that require more targeted analysis, independent working and delivering specific components of the bigger picture. Some will like a mixture of both. What is key to remember is that even in roles that you love; you need to be open to learning. Things are changing fast. You will need to have a willingness to keep learning and improving so that you can keep up with the pace of change.

Developing yourself:

If you are not strong in a particular area, it can always be changed with effort. It starts with a firm decision in your heart and mind, followed by a plan and time-bound actions to move you from a place of weakness to a place of building up your knowledge. Find out what you need to know and decide to invest time and practise to develop in that area. Also, don't let that process drag on. Just commit to hit it hard and to finishing it by a particular date. Shut everything else off and get it done.

Do the course. Read the book. Take on the work task in that area you don't like, then spend the hours to deliver something of quality. For job-related development, you can check in with other colleagues who regularly work in that space, but don't over depend on them to deliver it for you or you will not develop. Once you overcome the "hate it" hurdle, you need to keep up the practice so that, as you get more familiar with it, the new skill will become easier to do. You may even start to enjoy it.

Don't waste time! Of course, focusing your mind and energy to get to the end outcome by yourself is very rewarding. You learn from your mistakes and pick-up new skills. This is all excellent but if you can get there faster, do it. If there are others who have done it before you, ask them for help or just replicate their approach and copy their good example. It's not cheating or stealing. It's called being smart and efficient with the resources and people you have around you. The official term here is *learning from best practice* and then replicating it. Learn from the good examples that surround you. Do as they do. Make time to have training or coaching from them.

As you hear people around you or when you are dialled into calls or meetings, you can learn a lot from active listening, not just hearing noise, but actively listening for nuggets that will give you leads on further research that you can do. You are likely to have to read around your subject: read strategy papers, functional instruction manuals, newspapers. Speak to your more senior colleagues to get clear on what your gaps are and then make a learning plan.

Another thing to do is follow your organisation on LinkedIn and set up a news alert for your company and the key topics for your business area. You can then share interesting articles with your manager to pass on to the team. This demonstrates your industry awareness and is a great way to make wider contributions to the team. Be selective about what you share: high quality, current and relevant information from reputable sources.

Set a goal – smash it!

Make sure it is SMART – specific, measurable, achievable, realistic and time-bound (in a month).

Break the one-month goal down into tasks that need to be done, put them in order and schedule time in your life to complete the tasks. Put these into a diary, calendar, phone, notepad or efficiency app. Be committed to it. Make it realistic, take breaks as needed and include gaps for time with family and friends, etc.

An easy goal-setting example:

The goal is a professional qualification to be achieved in a month. That means completing sixteen modules and doing an exam to get a qualification – so this is you assessing what is involved to reach that goal. First, you break it down into smaller goals under the overall goal, with deadlines - four modules to be completed each week and in the last week, a revision slot and test slot to be added to the diary. Then break it down to actual tasks. Work out how long it will take to do each module - one hour each - and when you can do them.

Could be: Tuesday and Thursday evenings after work, two to be completed each night - that's four modules to hit each week. Every Tuesday and Thursday for that month, the actual modules for each evening go into your calendar as appointments. Tuesday and Thursday become working late days for that month, an extra two hours to finish the modules. In that final week, you may decide to take a day off for the final revision and exam which would also go into your calendar. By the end of the month, you take the test, and you pass. You achieve your SMART goal and make yourself more valuable.

To achieve goals, you will have to sacrifice some things right now for a set time period. If you don't, you will miss the target. The target continues to be something in front of you that needs to be achieved, rather than being behind you and pushing you forward now that you have conquered it. Putting things off wastes valuable time, keeps you stalled. Time = life. Wasting time is wasting life. Time is so precious. Make it count.

At the start, there is so much learning to be done. In every job, this is the case, even if you enter with great experience from a previous role, or with insights from study. When you aren't confident about your work, or you are unsure about what you are doing, it is important to just focus on filling that information or skills gap to avoid making a costly mistake. The following checklist will always be helpful, especially at the start of a role:

- Gather the key reading, strategy papers that you need and develop your knowledge of the area that you are responsible for, and the other business areas you work with or support.

- Find a buddy in your current role who can show you the ropes. Learn and carefully observe what they are doing, then practise yourself and adopt their winning approaches.

- Do a course, or hire a trainer, if there is a need to build technical skills like Excel, Programming, Data Analysis or Project Management for example. Do that early on to enhance your speed of delivery and the quality of your work.

- Look at your bigger targets and just like the goal setting summary above, break down those bigger targets into goals to hit over a 1, 2- or 3-month period. If they are not finished, DON'T start new projects or work until you have completed what you set out to complete.

If you start new goals without finishing the ones you previously set for yourself, very quickly, unfinished tasks can start to build up. As your time gets spread more thinly, it can leave you with too much to do in the time that you have. The effect of this - which I suffered many times - is not being able to deliver an output for all of the tasks on your list, or not delivering your highest standard of work. There is also the risk of getting very overwhelmed or missing deadlines. Your focus must be on having a manageable list and committing to finishing tasks/activities, before adding new ones.

Assessing your progress

When you have your quarterly review, if you have not achieved those things you set out to do, take these actions:

- Revise the goal and focus on the new target. You can't keep missing deadlines.

- Set a more realistic target if the time you previously gave yourself was too short.

- If the deadline was missed because of poor time management – wasting time – you have to commit mentally to achieving it. Be determined. Nobody will do this for you.

- Ask yourself: What do you need to say no to, to keep you focused? What will help you get it done?

- If you give up on the goal/idea completely and leave it unfinished, you will potentially regret it later, when the opportunity is gone, or someone else does it successfully. It's your choice.

So now let me share the story of a colleague I saw put this all into practice. This guy fully caught me by surprise when he joined. He had a strategy and a whole action plan for success worked out. His career progress was his number one focus and I found that out when he became my manager after just six months in the role. I learnt a lot from his approaches which I think will help you, too, but I think he could have been more skilful in the way he managed entering a new team, and team dynamics. I will pick up on that in the following chapter but for now, here is his story.

CHAPTER 8

CASE STUDY – *BOSSING IT*

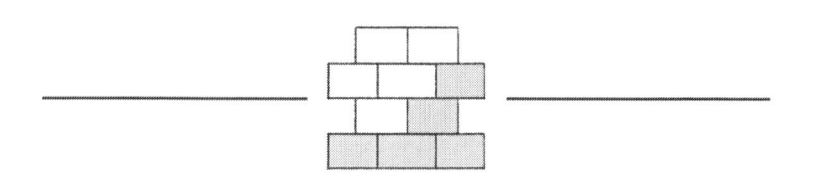

PAUL (NOT HIS REAL NAME) was a guy who landed in one of my teams. Within six months, he had made his first job move and in four years I watched him make three job moves with his pay being increased each time. Now, that is very rapid. In that same time, I had just about made one and a half moves. I learnt a lot from him and share his story to pass on wisdom nuggets that can be very beneficial for progress, as well as highlight some behaviours that are not recommended or necessary for progress.

He joined as a brand-new colleague about a year after I had joined the team. As I continued to comfortably hold onto the main skills I was known for, staying in my comfort zone, this guy came with his transferable skills and an attitude for acceleration. Within a month, by applying himself to reading about the role in his own time, being focused on team catch-ups and filling in the information gaps, he became the guy who had more in-depth technical knowledge than I did!

He came in on a mission. He had a strategy and that was to learn as much as he could and demonstrate his capabilities as soon as possible. He was stretching and challenging himself so he could add more value and gain recognition from our manager. He had so much focus and was so nice and helpful to everyone, so we all liked him, too. In general, I aim to be good to the people around me, so I thought he was just a nice person.

Within two months, however, he had fully milked all the information I had; and with his transferable skills and the new knowledge he had intentionally acquired through personal study, coffee catch-ups with colleagues, he skilled-up so rapidly that he even started helping me to understand my own business area! Within three months, he had identified areas for improvement and created a structured plan which my manager reviewed and approved. He began leading a project in my area, delivering outputs ahead of time and to a high standard. Within six months he went from being my colleague to being my team leader. I could not believe it!

At the time, I did not connect his development with his diligence. The following lessons I learnt were from watching him. Take note!

1. He operated with structure and was focused on going somewhere.
2. He was sparing with words, friendly and part of team banter but did not just talk for the sake of talking. He was

forming relationships and working hard at the same time. After building connections and working out what he needed to know, he committed to learning and adding value.

3. He listened attentively, watched carefully, and kept note of all the new information he was coming across. He was focused on rapidly progressing from where he had started in our team, and revised the business instruction manuals, so he fully understood them. Each week he seemed to be getting sharper and sharper, whilst I was just depending on what I was good at; not really committing to learning or venturing into the more technical aspects I did not find as easy. Very soon he began to be trusted to take on more responsibility. He always delivered tasks with quality and ahead of time.

4. Before jumping into a task, he would always assess it. Is it a priority? Who does it benefit? How critical is it? Can someone else do it? Do I need to create instructions, or a framework to go alongside it? Then he would work with sense and deliver quality.

Now one thing that began to frustrate me was the way he would communicate to our managers about the work we did together. He began to use "I" instead of "we" on things we had both worked on. He would somehow convert our joint effort into *his* effort. After a few too many instances, I began to wake up. It was the moment I realised that within a team, when it starts to become more competitive, it can become unfriendly, and less collaborative actions can begin to arise. Watch out for that.

I had to start being more proactive about mentioning my specific contributions to managers, especially on the things we were working on together.

In addition to claiming credit for "our" work, as his technical skills became stronger than mine, his confidence began to rise and a sense of arrogance. It wasn't long before I started to resent him. I felt he was a glory hunter, self-promoting, and I couldn't deny he was really good at what he did. He was so focused on being better and recognised. I had never seen anyone work in such an individualistic way. I grew up learning that teamwork and everyone helping each other as far as possible was important. I expected all teams and colleagues to operate like that in the world of work, but his way of working highlighted that people will not always collaborate and at any point can become very self-interested and forget the team.

A collaborative and helpful environment should exist, but you will also come across those who are focused on doing a great job individually and progressing rapidly. In reality, it's about balance, as both of these aspects are important. Though I became increasingly frustrated by him, now looking back, despite approaches that could have been more collegiate, I must admit he was truly *woke at work*. He knew how to shine and position himself for promotion. While I was still asleep, sluggishly developing, he was bossing it in his job because he had a goal and had implemented the strategy for winning.

His way of working and results, caused me to seriously examine why we were operating so differently. I realised:

- I was surviving on a set of skills that I had learnt and had no appetite to learn more.

- I believed I did not have to start again from scratch, and that basic details were unimportant.

- I was unintentional about my career and development. No plan. Took each day as it came.

- I had become comfortable, lazy. I wasted time, valuable time, as he rapidly progressed.

His level of confidence in terms of presenting himself was so clear and defined. He had learnt these skills early from private school and further developed at his elite university. He was then moulded and refined even further through a graduate scheme at one of the leading global consultancy firms. We had completely different journeys and that put us in completely different leagues though we were in the same team. I had seen real struggle on my way into the corporate world and was just grateful for my job and wanted to stay employed.

He was his CV. He was so confident about what he had to offer, he understood the organisational needs and how he could help solve problems. He was presenting himself from a place of abundance, knowing his value, his previous experience and what he could offer the organisation. This was a very different position from where I was coming from: "I need a job. Please hire me," or "I'm not sure of how much I can offer and really don't want to lose my job." Both statements give off the needy, scarcity mindset that doesn't present confidence but rather a sense of lack. Don't fall into that trap! Managers are always looking at who in their team can be trusted to deliver on tasks and add value. Honest abundance mindset all the way!

At that time, so early in my career, I wanted the shortcut to knowledge, feeling that much of what was around me was too hard to invest the time and endure the short-term pain and sacrifice to make progress. I initially held onto the fact that I had been there for longer than him, and heavily depended on my core skills that were getting me by. I focused on what enabled me to do my job and concentrated on protecting my position, and being celebrated for the standard activities expected from my job. What I did not realise was that to stay relevant and recognised, you need to take the responsibility to grow yourself. If not, you quickly go from being the new shiny thing to becoming rusty and even redundant. May that not happen to you! Drive yourself. Find out for yourself what you don't know and aim to fill those gaps.

> **Wisdom nugget:**
>
> *Time really does fly. Don't waste it. Remain in development and preparation mode. The more intentional you are about that, the more ready you will be to grab new opportunities.*

That is the end of his story, but there were lots of things to learn from it. He was someone who made himself visible and knew how to make sure the managers and influential stakeholders knew what he was contributing to the team. Reviewing the whole story, I can see a few points that Paul could have improved on to ensure that the team dynamic developed more collaboratively and positively with his teammates, in line with his achievements. This brings us to the next section, where I will be addressing the *way* you enter a team in more detail. There is an optimal attitude, energy, and approach you can have that builds rapport with those around you. The next chapter is filled with strategies to help you integrate smoothly and accelerate within teams, ensuring that you also have more supporters around you than enemies.

PART THREE

FRAMEWORK FOR SUCCESS

Set things in motion

CHAPTER 9

NEW TEAM - DYNAMICS AND STRATEGIES

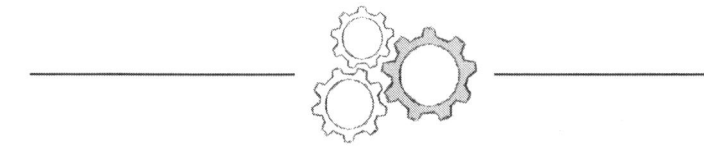

WHEN YOU JOIN A NEW TEAM, although many people are usually supportive, some may see you as a threat. Others may see you as a burden, as you will need to be trained and upskilled. Some may just have no interest in you at all, and others will be gems – great colleagues who just want to help you settle. The gems will give you their time and insight and maybe show you the path to follow. With such people, you should take the opportunity for support and connecting upfront if offered. If you have knowledge gaps in the new area, it is good to stay connected to these people, to learn from and ask questions. Be careful to manage the amount of their time you take up. One or two meetings in a week is okay. Don't overuse their willingness to help.

Though everything is rapidly digitising, there may be more screen use to connect with your colleagues, but you will still be working with people, so be mindful of their personalities and the ways that they work. Be intentional about how you come across. Please take note of the following steps to help you settle into your new role safely:

1. Don't come in as a threat - even if you are the new manager or taking over a person's job!

2. Respect those who were there before you. Respect their knowledge and take their opinion. Get your new team members onside early. Be humble when you approach things, as they are the ones with the knowledge, and you are the one wanting to learn and help where you can. This approach is non-threatening and secures their willingness to help you, rather than making them feel challenged by you. Get them onside early!

3. Look for ways that you can collaborate on existing work and help colleagues succeed. Learn and build your reputation as a team player.

4. Ask as many questions as you can in the first two months; that is usually the grace period given to new joiners.

5. Do your own back-up study and research, so you can demonstrate knowledge and gain more value. There will be investor day presentations and strategy papers that tell you about the organisation and the key priorities – read and understand how your world fits into that.

6. Don't skip the foundations. Build the base set of skills that you will need for the role and fill any gaps you have at the beginning. Tasks or learning may seem boring or basic but the earlier you bag core knowledge or skills that are key to your area, the further you will fly as you have the foundation knowledge to approach the more challenging work.

7. Don't ridicule things you don't agree with or boast about how much better another place is in comparison. It's too early for you to start criticising when you have just joined. If you do, you will become a target - possibly creating enemies.

8. Use the early weeks to observe and personally take note of areas of improvement, then identify your space/opportunity to add value and be recognised – this is an ongoing activity.

9. Ask for key reading materials to build your business knowledge and technical skills.

When you are new, making an impact and doing well is key. If you really shine early on, there can sometimes be hostility from teammates whom you are outperforming. This comes from them feeling insecure because of how well you are doing so quickly. It stems from jealousy. It may not happen overtly but in some cases, where people feel threatened by a person who has come in all guns blazing with new ideas and processes, they can be unhelpful at best, and an enemy of progress at worst. Behaviours such as pettiness, not sharing information, allowing you to fail publicly and gathering others against you can happen, though it is rare. To avoid this, an attitude of humility and of being a team player, and someone committed to building collaborative relationships is the best approach. Follow steps 1-3 intentionally and you will avoid issues.

Energy levels when entering a new team are important. You need to aim for the right balance of interest and energy. I am naturally an extrovert and when I am excited, I can be a perceived to be full FORCE. When I'm operating at full drive, I have a lot of energy. Powerful and captivating has been the usual response, but high energy people can be overwhelming. If you are an extrovert, try and balance the release of your energy carefully, gradually at first, and then released as you get to know people.

In contrast, if you are an introvert, you will have to make the extra effort to step out of your space and proactively make your introductions across the team. Be willing to connect and make the first move to introduce yourself, so that your presence and role are acknowledged. At the very least, you should be willing to ask for help to get up to speed and ask for any support you need – don't suffer in silence.

Whatever your personality type or tendencies, the safest approach when starting a new role is to enter calmly, with a professional and friendly manner. This eases you in gently and you should then work on understanding the personalities and dynamics of the team that you are in. Just enter the situation visibly interested in your new role and focus on integrating within the team.

Success is how quickly you can feel part of the team and have a handle on what is going on, and what you are there to do.

You need to keep learning. There will be brand new things that you will need to upskill in. Here is a suggestion of what information to acquire in the first month. These are things to be intentional about understanding.

People mapping

- Who is the most senior person? You need to land a good first impression with them.

- At your level, who seems to know everything? Your first questions/upskilling starts here.

- Who does everyone go to for help? This is a good person to know as possible support when you are in need; they are likely to be personable, too.

- Who is the most popular person? Be careful. Why are they popular? Get to understand them. They may become territorial, not wanting competition or they may just be great. Assess.

- Who seems genuine/fun? This could be a friend if you are open to friendships at work.

Getting up to speed within the business

Week one – There is going to be a lot of basic admin. This is a low value add but you need to know it. This is likely to be very boring and mundane. Just get it done. The sooner it is ticked off, you can move onto growing in the areas that you were hired to impact. Get a hold of the overall business area information, get an organisational chart about the key people, areas and what they do, get all your access and mandatory training done, watch or read recent strategic releases from the business – these are all important.

Week two – Read strategy papers, speak to more senior colleagues and schedule informal catch-ups to get to know people in person or virtually.

Week three – Learn the industry background, business priorities and the main targets for the business.

Week four – Set up a meeting with your boss to confirm the priorities you need to focus on and deliverables.

Initial meet-ups/coffees/lunches

There will be a lot of new people to meet – be intentional about getting to know them. It is important that you start off being approachable. Arrange catch-ups with team members if they have not proactively set up a time with you. In some teams, you may not always be invited for lunch/coffee so make the first move. Be brave! Invite new team members to lunch or coffee and purposely get to know them.

If you have asked someone to give you some time to explain something to you, even if it is at the beginning, it will be a time for you to just get a download of key information. If you have been in the role for a while and need to get further information to understand areas more deeply, then you can be more targeted in what you need from your time together. In both scenarios, write down beforehand what you want to get out of the session.

Always have your notepad with you. Write down the subject of the meeting, date, and person you spoke to. Have a targeted approach to the time you have with them. After initial niceties, give an overview of what you want to understand and then go through your prepared list. As they share against each one, update each point at the end of the session; it will be more than just a coffee catch-up. You will know that you have achieved an objective. You will have that information you need as a reference point and that you won't have to repeat your request for help.

Here's a list of things you can ask about:

- Their career background and how long they have been in the team?
- What area do they work in and how is that connected to your world?
- What are their priorities?

Just listen and learn; that is the purpose of these initial meetings. If you don't have a clear idea of what you want from the meeting, some people will just bombard you and the session will not go in a clear direction because they know so much, and you have no way to filter for relevant information.

Don't be too quick to offer help even if things have been said that excite you. At best, say something like, "I have experience in that area. It would be good to delve deeper at some point." Don't commit yourself for tasks during these initial discovery meetings because you are one person meeting a whole new team. Over-promising to help everyone sounds great to those you are making promises to and will make you feel helpful. The problem is, by you saying "yes" too quickly, you may end up overcommitting yourself and not being able to deliver. Or you may end up missing deadlines because you have taken on too much. If that happens, your brand will be impacted, and your integrity will be hit early on.

This over-promising and under-delivering is a risk, which could affect your reputation before you have had a chance to prove yourself. People's trust in your ability and your reliability could then be damaged. If this happens repeatedly over time as you progress in the role, it can result in the more strategic, high visibility work not being given to you because managers depend on being able to trust employees to deliver what they need when they need it. It can be a challenge to turn things back into your favour and reset their view of you if doubt sets in about your ability to deliver. So only say "yes" when you know you can do it. A better response is, "Let me check what I have on currently and get back to you." Or ask, "When do you need it by?" You can then try and work out a realistic plan. Being helpful shows team support. Just be wise with it.

Now in the next chapter, the focus will be on how you intentionally work on being visible in your role. In the *Bossing It* case study, we read about Paul who ensured that those managers around him knew what he was doing and the value he was contributing. Managing your output to a high standard and being visible as someone who delivers results, is very important. Now we will look at how you can proactively work on being visible in your roles and ensure that key stakeholders are aware of what you are doing and the value you are contributing.

CHAPTER 10

BEING VISIBLE - SPOTLIGHT AND SHINE

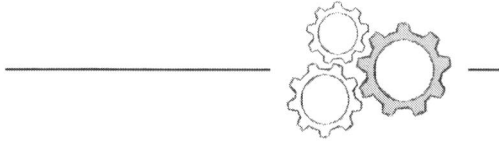

VISIBILITY! THIS CONCEPT IS SO KEY. Right from the start of my career I worked in roles that were strategic to the business area I was in. I was operating in very high visibility spaces but I didn't even know what visibility was, or how to use it to my advantage. Visibility is working on things that showcase what you can do in front of interested senior business stakeholders, and the work and your involvement results in more exposure for you. Having visibility is like PR in your job. It is about being in the view of your managers in a way that can influence your progress and access to opportunities.

The most basic form of visibility is just being seen and recognised for what you are doing at work, but that's pretty low level as everyone is *seen* in their role. The best visibility is working on anything your manager, or the business really care about. Things that everyone is watching closely to be successful. That definitely comes with added pressure, but if great outcomes are achieved, great rewards follow.

Visibility can also be influenced by you directly. Having periodic catch-ups with your manager to let him or her know what you are working on, and the value you are bringing is very important for building your brand. You could send your manager a weekly bullet point summary of what you have achieved and what you will be focused on in the upcoming week. This is really organised, and you can then pull those emails together during your career conversations. Stronger than that is visibility through exposure.

Exposure happens when you actively take on work that more senior colleagues/managers are monitoring, care about, need, or when you are being put on special priority projects. This type of work is sometimes more strategic than operational and depends on your relationship with your manager. If good, you can discuss it during a career review chat and request to support or be put forward for work on more strategic projects. If not so good, focus on delivering really great work and gathering feedback from those who have benefitted. This feedback should then be packaged in an email, stating what you have delivered, and the benefits to your stakeholders.

In the opposite way, if you just isolate yourself, quietly working on your tasks, avoiding meeting with your manager, then what you are doing can't be seen. This just means you will have to do a lot more work alone to progress upwards, as you are less likely to be at the front of their mind when conversations arise about opportunities and suitable candidates. Another caution is that if the redundancy axe starts swinging, and without a strong performance record backed up by feedback and visibility, you can't defend yourself at the last minute. Your manager and stakeholders should know that you have been doing a great job on an ongoing basis. Don't slack on that. Work hard. Get written feedback. Share it. Stay visible.

With the feedback you receive, the best approach is to forward it on to your managers for awareness, although sometimes it can seem pretentious or boastful to do so. It is not. Sending feedback upward is just how it works and what is expected. This positive feedback helps you to easily build your brand through word-of-mouth recommendation. It's less about who you know and more about who knows you. Many of my job moves came from a recommendation: someone in a more powerful position above me who knew about me and my capabilities. I was visible to them on projects, in teams and from what they saw - they would then decide if they wanted me to consider taking on another job.

In some cases, managers have spoken on my behalf and put in a great word for me or because they knew what I was capable of, I have been offered roles. In such cases, trust is involved in your selection, so you really have to commit to delivering results against the potential seen in you.

Your visibility and exposure are important, so work on how you can showcase your work and capability authentically without boasting.

Where you are working with more than one manager, make sure that all are aware of what you are doing. If your work will directly support the managers above your manager, you can arrange a catch-up and share how you are progressing. The more you are known by several managers for your great work, the more likely it is that those managers will have you on their mind when opportunities arise that require your skills. They may then mention you when other managers are looking for a suitable candidate, and on the other extreme if there are discussions about needing to make people redundant you are more likely to be protected.

As your role progresses beyond your manager or immediate team, it is wise to have a person who understands your work environment and can give you appropriate and valuable advice. This person can be called upon when challenging situations arise or when you just need guidance. This is a mentor - a person with a good professional track record, inspirational to you and ideally someone who isn't directly connected to your business area so that you can speak freely with them. Usually, this is someone willing to listen, who shows care or interest in you - sounds a bit like a workplace counsellor, which it can be at times. These people can be very helpful / instrumental. In the next chapter, we will look at the different types of mentors you can have at work and how to build, maintain and respect your relationship with them.

CHAPTER 11

MENTORS AT WORK

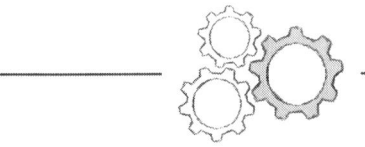

SHARING A WORK PROBLEM OR SITUATION with the right person can halve it, in the same way that sharing the problem with the wrong person can multiply it.

The Cambridge English dictionary simply defines a mentor as *"a person who gives a younger or less experienced person help and advice over a period of time."* As you read in the opening chapter, the first mentor I had was instrumental in preparing me for the job roles that came up during that first year after university and helping me secure an amazing role. In the Bible, it says, "In the multitude of wise counsel, there is safety." Mentors are the wise counsel that you need at work. In my experience, I have seen them fall into two categories, which I have defined below.

Business focused mentors – Those who have very limited time. They are very senior and business focused. They will give you a strategy for your career development. They can sometimes be called your *career mentor* and you need to jot down all they tell you. They make a commitment that you can trust them, but usually, you are connecting on a purely professional level. With such mentors. When they have agreed to be a mentor to you. Arrange sessions and make sure you focus on your objective for the conversation and what you need to know. Ask them a focused set of questions and specifics that you need clarity on.

Relational mentors - This is a term I have coined for those mentors who are more invested in you as a person. They may be more willing to form a deeper relationship, opening up more about personal experiences and also providing motivation and encouragement. These are the types of mentors who have become like friends or guardians at work, colleagues or managers who really want you to do well and are there to help you navigate tricky teams, mistakes and approaches to challenging situations at work. The mentoring relationship tends to have a more personal connection. With such mentors, when they have agreed to mentor you, make time with them, and though you should still have an objective for your meeting time, you often can share in more detail than the more distant purely business focused mentors.

You can also find mentors by connecting with people you work with, who inspire you and can guide you on how to develop your role. They would be your *in role* mentors. Managers or colleagues more senior to you, with whom you have a good relationship and who understand you as a person. Usually, two *in role* mentors are enough so that there aren't too many people involved in your development conversations aside from your manager. These may even be managers or colleagues that you worked with previously who really invested in you. There are also official company mentoring programmes in some organisations that you can sign up to and connect with managers wanting to mentor. That approach guarantees that person already wants to support a mentee.

People usually say "yes" when asked to be a mentor. It is something of an honour to be asked, but you should then ensure you make the most of it, setting up the catch-ups and making sure you implement what you agreed to do. Take time to put together a career development plan so you have something concrete to focus your conversations around, as your mentor will likely be asking about your career aspirations, where you see yourself in future and your goals. We pick up on this in detail in chapter 18. Having the updated document demonstrates you are proactive and prepared - raising the connection from a casual catch-up to one that has something that has a focused conversation.

As you progress through your role, issues may arise that are harder to deal with by yourself. Reaching out to your mentor for advice and guidance is very likely to help you avoid making mistakes. When you are struggling in a role, speak to your mentor about strategies to overcome. Speak to your mentor about your strengths and interests. Ask them for advice on what to focus on to enhance your development and impact.

When you are thinking about going for a new role, reach out to your mentor for advice on how to approach it and how to position yourself for the interview or the hiring manager. There are so many ways that a mentor can help you be the best version of yourself and wisely approach situations you have never experienced before. They leverage their past experiences and give you their wisdom. Agree how regularly they are able to catch-up and then you set up the meeting. Monthly is usually a good interval.

Before your meetings, prepare what you want to discuss. Things will arise in between your sessions as you get on with your job. Make a note of these things to discuss or get advice on, so that you can take them to your mentoring sessions and work on solutions. Plan before you meet so you have a more focused and productive conversation. Take notes and work on what you have agreed after the meeting. Your mentor seeing you take action after your meeting, presents you in a responsible way.

If an emergency comes up, you can reach out to your relational mentors, but as a mentee don't over depend on your mentor's time or help. Use their time wisely. Time = Life. Time can be wasted and in the same way, life can therefore be wasted. When people give you their time, they are sacrificing it for you. Value that. Value their investment in you.

When you are together focus your conversation. Use what you get from them and use it as far as possible before you need to go back to them again. As you are implementing their advice, you can reach out if any new outcome occurs which would require additional advice on how best to navigate that. It will show your mentor that you have taken their advice, and this outcome has developed from progressing their guidance so they will usually be willing to commit to helping you see it through to the end.

Time wasters or lazy people will take valuable time from a mentor and not plan before a meeting. Never operate like that. They usually end up going over the time period allocated for the meeting, they are unprepared, and the conversation then lacks focus. They don't take down the notes from what they are told and then constantly go back to ask for help without committing to implementing change. If you are a good investment, people realise that when they invest time in you - it produces a greater return and they are willing to invest more time in you. Commit to being a good investment using what you have been given to learn, be better and then give your mentor feedback on how their advice helped - this will really give them a boost.

Mentoring can also happen in reverse and more junior colleagues can give some great advice or feedback. Let your pride go and be open to guidance from everywhere. Perspectives are everything. Filter for what you need but don't put up a wall to information. Many intelligent and insightful people are coming up through the generations who maybe haven't faced the same things you may have, so their "can do, go for it" attitude can be so helpful for motivating more senior colleagues out of a rocky place.

If you are a mentor to someone at an earlier stage of their career, be careful about the amount of time you invest in mentoring. There is SO much value in helping someone up the ranks and it makes you feel good but again, manage the amount of time you give, especially as a young mentor under thirty. As you also are developing so that you can be even more inspirational to those coming after you, make sure that you carefully manage your time if you are mentoring others.

I recommend that you have at least one relational and one business-focused mentor. They are a valuable and necessary source of guidance to support you through your work. Now that we have looked at mentors and mentoring, in the next chapter we will look at another important contact who can significantly help with your progress at work: Sponsors.

CHAPTER 12

SPONSORS HELP YOU MOVE – WATCH OUT FOR MOTIVES

A SPONSOR IS DIFFERENT FROM A MENTOR. These are often very senior people who also have influence over job roles because of their seniority and network. They are people within your organisation or network of contacts that may be connected to an area you are interested in. If they put in a good word for you, their support can open doors to new job roles by putting you in a favoured position with recruiters or hiring managers. To be your sponsor they will need to know you, so you will have worked on being visible to them, building a relationship over time and they will therefore know what you are capable of. They will have seen your work, or you may have worked on a project for them and done a really great job. These are the people you meet less frequently but scheduling a periodic catchup to update them on what you are doing and what you want to be doing is very important, that is how you build the relationship and let them know you are someone desiring to be progressed and open to new opportunities.

Timing is very important. Usually, the sponsor conversation happens when you are ready for a role change, you have a strong track record and you have an idea of where you want to move. At that point, you will need to be bold and ask to have a catch-up discussion with them. At the catch-up, talk about the great things you are working on and let them know about your desire to move into a more senior role that would enable you to add more value. Ask for their advice first, and then end by asking for their support if you come across any suitable roles. They will give you advice and tell you what they can do.

They are the people who can put a good word in for you during a recruitment process, and even tell the hiring manager that they support your application and give it more weight. This may seem very strange, but it really is an important part of how job moves often happen in the workplace. This is a more professional version of someone saying "I know someone who would be great for this" and telling the manager why they support the person.

If a sponsor agrees to support you, your commitment must be to do the job to the best of your ability in the new role. They are investing their good word and reputation in you.

Now as a point of caution, if you share an opportunity that does not support the sponsor's business area, then you have really gone to them in a mentoring capacity. It is better to have such conversations with a mentor outside your business area. If a sponsor is hearing that you are thinking of leaving their business area, their advice might be more aligned to what is in the best interests of their business area - this is something you need to be mindful of. The advice should be about helping you to be the best that you can be. You will always have to weigh up your options on what you hear.

Like the example shared at the beginning of this book, the manager I looked to as a sponsor gave me the advice to let go of the opportunity that I had been presented with and stay within their department. The manager promised me so much that was in the future, whereas I was being offered a new job elsewhere which was real. It was a promotion, pay rise and move to a new company. In that case, I spoke to a lot of people as I did not want to affect the relationship by taking a different option to what the manager had advised. I also had to pray about it to reach the final decision, which eventually was to detach emotionally and follow the opportunity.

In another case, I had an opportunity outside my sponsor's area. I had a conversation with them seeking advice out of courtesy, as we had a close working relationship. In a similar way, I was asked not to take the role and stay; the sponsor then assured me about some opportunities and benefits that would be secured for me in the future. In that case, I heard their advice and promises. I also spoke to trusted people and mentors who were not connected to my business area and only had my best interest at heart.

Some of them shared the same faith so after listening to my many deliberations, they also prayed about the whole thing with me, too. In the end, that was the trigger. I got my clarity and experienced the highest level of peace about not pursuing the opportunity which, on its face value, seemed amazing. Just a few months after I had turned down the role, I found out that all structures surrounding that job literally crumbled. As amazing as the role sounded, it was a move that would have been very detrimental to me if I had taken it. It would have been the wrong decision. Talk about being saved!

I realised the importance of speaking to sponsors when a role came up in their area. They often have insight into whether it is a good move for you or whether there may be a better option. You then need to take away what you have heard and weigh it up, make a list of the pros and cons of the new role vs. staying where you are. Spend this time to analyse your options will really help you to get the assurance you need inside to make your decision. The choice is yours to make, not that of the sponsor or mentor. Though their roles can be very significant in helping with your progress, decide what is best, with the information and support you have available to you. Be brave, ask for what you want.

We are now going to look at the range of discoveries to proactively manage your career progression. For so long I was just floating along, hoping for the best. That strategy kept me in a job, but it was when I heard stories of how others were progressing and handling their review meetings that my mindset shifted. New levels of planning and goal setting were required. I had to start actively managing my career. After I had spent three years in a role, I was in a conversation with a colleague who shared that after about eighteen months you should be in a position to start looking for a new job.

That felt so sudden to me at the time and I began to reflect on different scenarios around me. Some people were comfortable where they were and there was no desire to push to more senior positions perceived as more demanding and stressful. Others had tried multiple times to progress with no success and had given up on trying. There were definitely those that were rapidly advanced but that was less common. I thought about what I was capable of and decided that I wanted to progress further. I knew I had what it took to be in more senior positions and to manage more responsibility. I realised I had become comfortable, staying in the safe world of what was familiar and easy to do. The decision to progress was made but it definitely was not easy. If you want to progress, you have to put in extra work, manage your performance, be clear on the value that you are delivering and communicate it. Most importantly be resilient – never give up. Disappointments may come but you have to keep pushing for opportunities, keep building your brand and develop the key relationships that can support you to advance your career.

In the next chapter, we delve into part two of team dynamics and focus on strategies to deal with situations where it starts to get competitive, or your work is at a higher or lower level than others in your team. How do you manage those dynamics and the human, emotional reactions and actions that can be triggered? I journeyed through many of these experiences and share practical guidance on how you approach with caution and avoid tension. Let's go!

CHAPTER 13

TEAM DYNAMICS PART 2 - COMPETITION AND PROGRESS

IT'S IMPORTANT TO COLLABORATE, but never forget how you come across and what you personally bring to the table. Make sure your managers know what you are doing specifically so that your contribution to the team is being recognised. As a teammate and colleague, it is the expectation to work with colleagues and feed into the support of the team. It is also important to be able to share your work so you will not be seen as coasting along or riding on the coattails of others.

When you are in a team and you start being recognised repeatedly for work you are doing, this can lead to you being given more responsibilities or even the opportunity to start leading your teammates. This shift can cause friction if not handled with care. Jealousy and unwillingness to be led by someone who was previously just your colleague can arise in the minds of your teammates. To avoid this, don't be arrogant or domineering. Humbly and progressively take on the new responsibility. Focus on doing what you need to do to successfully deliver in your role. Continue to be helpful to your teammates as far as possible, celebrating others and supporting team development. Lead where you are asked to and don't boast about personal praise you're receiving. Send feedback upwards to your managers/sponsors that need to know. Maintain harmony in your team dynamic and remove the risk of tension growing, especially in small teams.

Now if it becomes apparent that your manager isn't as good as their role requires and you can see a better way of working, this should be a signal that you are developing the capabilities to do your manager's role. Sometimes, managers above your manager may see your talent and development before your own manager acknowledges it. This can happen because your manager may view you as their junior and want to protect their more senior role. In such cases, it can start to feel like them trying to keep you where you are. So be careful in this situation.

If seniors above your manager are reaching out for you directly, the best thing is to funnel things through your manager but keep up your direct connections with those more senior managers, too. They have spotted you so you can build on that and find out if there are opportunities for you to step up. In such a scenario, the wrong move is taking a decision to start trying to do your manager's job to show them what to do. You have not been given that responsibility. It will seem like you are undermining their authority and they are only going to feel threatened by that and then possibly become a barrier to your progress. It is better to respect their position and make suggestions to them on how to improve on how things are done and implemented. That feedback favours you personally and you can also mention these enhancements you have originated at your review meeting and with your mentors and sponsors.

A way that you can continue to develop a more senior level skillset, is by asking your manager for opportunities to support them. This would enable you to work more closely with them. You reduce their stress by helping them and you also learn about their job in the process. This is a great opportunity for your development. There are times when a manager can dump their work on you. This can feel very rude, especially in the way it is done but I would challenge you to see this as another great opportunity. Their laziness just gives you access to their work. You can learn what they are doing and develop the skills and get experience of their role. That then prepares you for opportunities at their level or even for their role if they move on.

Just be careful that you don't let yourself be overburdened and stressed by taking on too much work. You still have to be able to deliver quality and protect your brand. On the other side, if you have had too much work dumped on you and you become overwhelmed by it, you just need to say, "I don't have any more bandwidth. The increased workload has overstretched my capacity to deliver. Could we review my current workload and decide what things can be distributed so I can maintain my quality of output." These phrases all trigger that there is a problem.

Sometimes you have to be firm on this, as some managers can overburden you with a very heavy workload and start to behave like a bully so that you feel afraid to raise the issue with them. In such cases, evenings, weekends, and early mornings are then consistently being used to get it all done. No rest, high stress. You don't have to do this to yourself or accept their behaviour. You are an employee, not a slave. Raise the issue and ask them to look for a solution. They have options: the work goes to someone else or another team, they hire someone else, they do more of the work themselves, or they reduce the work.

Just remember that in every role, you will need to learn new things and you have to drive your own education, even when the resources are provided for you. You have access to most of the same information that is available to your manager, so see it as a time to learn even more about what you need for more senior roles. Actively observe the situations your manager is in and learn from that. Be more interested in developing your broader knowledge and then show your manager that your knowledge has increased and that you are willing to support with more. If a more senior opportunity comes up, you're then ready to convince stakeholders that you are the person for that job. Preparation is key. Assess yourself for the role above your role. What are the areas you are not able to do? Work on building your capabilities on top of the job you are currently doing.

Now one of the biggest and most common career progression mistakes is not putting enough focus on your personal career planning and performance management process. This is something of which you must take active ownership. The annual performance process happens within most if not all corporate organisations and the outcomes heavily influences how far one can progress. It is also the process that is most closely connected to the growth of your salary and benefits. Let's delve deeper.

PART FOUR

MANAGING YOUR CAREER

Make wise moves

CHAPTER 14

CAREER PLANNING – BEST PRACTICE

CAREER PLANNING IS A COMMON TERM, easy to understand and makes good sense. More common, however, is the lack of time employees actually spend on it. This most essential activity that gives direction to the time you spend at work, and intention to how you use your time, is often treated casually, or not even engaged with at all. Career planning is important. Do it. It is about spending focused time to concentrate on yourself - your goals and the vision you have for your career over a set period of time. It then enables you to put milestones in place and work towards achieving them.

Career planning does not need to be done at work. A great approach is to take out an afternoon a month, on a weekend to get away from everything else and focus on your plan. Typically, you will be looking at where you are now, the role you are targeting in the next two years, and the skills and experiences you need to obtain to help you develop towards that. This focused time, also helps you to assess if your current role is helping you work towards your goal. In this chapter, we will look at key career planning components and timelines and look in-depth at how you approach your career development plan.

As previously mentioned, between two to three years is usually the optimum time to be in a role to really obtain valuable experience, contribute enough to build up a reputation and personal brand, and increase your network of professional contacts in the role. Two years is not a hard and fast rule but is a good time to start considering the next move. At the start of a job, the first six months are for setting development targets, building your confidence, demonstrating the new and relevant information you have learnt, and working on creating impact through early successes and strong and consistent delivery.

The 6- to 12-month period is when the mid-year and end of year performance reviews happen with your managers. Now if you join in the middle of a year, say July, it is likely that your first cyclical performance review will be at the end of the year. What is most important is that you prepare. At these performance meetings your progress is discussed, your manager shares their expectations, and you agree on a plan for what you need to do to achieve the objectives for your role.

When you have been with an organisation for 12- to 18-months, you move into a period where you should aim to accelerate. Have stretch targets and focus on the big efforts you can make to demonstrate your value and capability. It is a great period to build on your hopefully strong performance and really impress. For every role, there are a set of objectives the company wants you to achieve. These are usually compiled to make up your personal scorecard.

SCORECARDS AND OBJECTIVES

A scorecard is what the business will be measuring your performance against during the year. Scorecards have shown up in my career journey and are common in the corporate world but in some organisations, it may be a set of objectives or *key performance indicators* (KPIs). These are a set of targets that you are usually given by your manager as key things to deliver and be measured against in your role. In some organisations, usually corporate world settings, these objectives are grouped together and the complete list is called your *employee scorecard*. At the end of the year, all the objectives and the targets you are expected to hit are assessed at your final/end of year performance review.

Each objective will usually have a title, a description, and a set of measures and targets to hit. At the start of the year, you usually agree your objectives with your manager. This is the beginning of your annual career planning process and should be taken seriously, especially your objectives and how well you achieve them, as this will determine how you are rated at the end of the year.

Your objectives will always be aligned to the overall goals of your business area and what your manager is responsible for.

Your objectives then should feed upwards into how your role helps your manager and your business area achieve their overall objectives. Your manager can then measure you on how you directly contribute to the overall objective of your business area. Your objectives should not be random or disconnected from what you are doing. They should be tailored to your actual work-goals and targets.

In some cases, they will be split into financial and non-financial objectives, which focus on what you are doing and what needs to be delivered in your role to meet the expectations of the business. In some cases, there are also behavioural objectives that focus more on your attitude and how you work. Your performance against what is on your scorecard/objectives/KPIs, usually determines your end of year performance ratings and what additional reward benefits you receive. What you deliver in your job and how you deliver against your objectives are taken into consideration.

Now sometimes, especially in large organisations, the objectives/KPIs are very general, so it is difficult to identify with them. Sometimes the objectives are created by the central or global business leadership team. These teams are more strategic and have a high-level view of what is expected from each of the business areas, and they compile high-level generic objectives to be achieved. These are then cascaded down to managers to share with their teams. Because of this, in some businesses the objective setting process can become vague, with a set of objectives that do not align to your specific role. If that is the case, you can make a request to your manager to adapt the generic objectives, so they are more specific to your role. It will therefore be important for you to proactively find out from your manager what their expectations are for your role and, specifically, how you will be measured.

Make sure your agreed objectives are updated officially in writing with your manager signing it (or have an email record of your agreed objectives if you cannot update an official HR system). Be clear on what your performance is being measured against. Include your stretch targets – the extra things you aim to achieve above your normal job to secure the higher measure of performance.

Now the objective setting process does usually happen at the start of the year but also at the start of your new role. Keep your focus on making sure you are working towards achieving your objectives and ensure you are aware of the measures of success/KPIs. That is what will give you the leverage to negotiate for more, development opportunities, a promotion or pay rise.

Take greater ownership for driving the progress when it comes to your career development. Whilst this should typically be a two-way process, you should not place the onus on your line manager for driving this forward. The reality is that while this is of great importance to you, this may not feature at the top of your manager's list of priorities and they may not proactively support you on that journey. Do it for yourself!

As the year progresses, keep track of your progress and achievements. Discuss them during your career catch-ups, at your mid-year review and at your year-end review. Usually, your manager will complete a feedback form on your performance, and you will complete your own self-assessment. This manager feedback along with your self-assessment is usually updated on the central HR system. End-of-year formal updates often happen a few months before the actual year end. As a result, be mindful that you should aim to hit your objectives and stretch targets within nine months, rather than leaving your performance effort to the last quarter of the year. There are some organisations where promotions are decided formally at points in the annual review cycle, so don't wait until the end of the year to showcase your best work.

When the final review of your performance is completed, you are given your end-of-year performance and behavioural ratings. There is usually a scale from good to not so good. I have seen a 5-point scale and some organisations adopt a simplified 3-point scale, or descriptions for performance such as outstanding to poor/under-performing. Just to give you an idea, I will use the 1 5point scale. The performance rating '1' usually denotes that your delivery far exceeds the required standard for your role; this would be used to identify those for promotion. Most employees achieve the middle '3' being good, operating as expected, whereas a '2' is very good and sometimes strong enough to support a promotion. '4/5' indicates issues in the role and would be a signal for HR to intervene and look at procedures to bring performance to an acceptable level.

In addition to the performance rating, as mentioned you may have behavioural ratings in your organisation, also on a scale.

Again, assuming a 1-5 scale, '1' - would be a role model, exemplary attitude and, again, suitable to lead/be promoted, whilst '4/5' shows a negative attitude/unprofessionalism, poor approach to work, and/or just a bad relationship with their boss. The '4/5' level rating is seen as serious and usually triggers formal warnings or *performance improvement plans* (PIPs).

PIPs are initiated by managers and can be monitored formally by HR. They are focused on rapidly driving improvement in performance and will have a firm set of targets set with warnings of job loss if significant improvement is not demonstrated. This whole process should be avoided as far as possible. Work on managing your role and relationships well to ensure any issue are raised and resolved, and you won't end up on a PIP. If you ever do cross into PIP territory, it will be time to *really* focus. Determine to take extra caution. Set personal targets that will stretch you and go for it! Prove that you should have never been put on it. For more on handling HR procedures and PIPs, see Chapter 26 later in the book.

Now we move from the objective setting phase into the next key part of your personal career planning – your actual career development plan. You are the creator and owner of this document. It is your career sidekick, and you are responsible for keeping it up to date as a tool for your career aspirations and targets. It is the document that is designed to help you focus on your progress, and where you are going; it requires you to step up your current level of working to achieve that higher level you desire. You create it and you must then hold yourself accountable to it. Nobody else can do that for you. It only matters to you and for you. If you don't give it the attention it requires, it dies. Don't let that happen. Let's explore this topic in more detail.

YOUR CAREER DEVELOPMENT PLAN

Your career development plan is a separate document that you personally create/update and manage. The document is all about you, your strengths, your areas for development and where you want to be in 2 to 3 years' and then in 3 to 5 years' time. It is about your personal development goals and career ambitions. You put what you want on the document to help you focus on how well you are progressing. In some roles, a proactive manager will encourage you to have one, and will want to see how you are personally progressing to develop yourself. In other cases, a manager may not be interested or may just be too busy to really engage with your personal development. For this reason, your plan is your own responsibility. If you don't maintain it and keep it alive to help focus your career progression and performance conversations, nobody else will.

For an effective career development plan, you need to have a section for your role now, your target role for the medium term – say in 2-3 years' time, and then your target role for the longer-term, say for 3-5 years' time and then +5 years. Now be careful with that because in some cases, your target role may be your manager's role. Please don't target your manager's role during your career development conversations - even if that would be an ideal role for you. You should position that kind of idea much more generally, something like - you would like to "move into more of a leadership role," "take on people management responsibilities," "management of more countries," "take more ownership of the reporting process," and not "I see myself in your role in 2 years."

Another section should be for skills that you want to specialise in. These are things you are good at that you want to become great at; again, targeting the medium term and the longer-term career goals that you want to achieve by then. What will you be wanting to tackle over the next 2-3 years and what will you want to take on after that? Be specific about the qualifications, training, development and experiences you aspire to achieve. Also, have a section for identifying the areas where development is required. Make a list and for each one, think about if it is needed in your job and for what you want to do in the future. Against each one put *essential/desirable.*

The ones that are *essential* you need to work on to improve. Your improvements will propel you further and faster. Not developing those essential skills will hamper your progress. For the other things that you are not good at that may have received a *not needed*, bear in mind that at the start of your career, there are many things that you may not like, but most skills need to be developed early on to give you the solid foundation to handle jobs in the corporate world. Honestly assess if anything is *desirable* and not linked to your job and the direction you want to go in the future. It is likely to only be a few things but for those things, don't waste time forcing yourself to be good at them. You have to focus on what will really strengthen you and what you can get really good at. With these weaker areas you should aim to get to an acceptable level or get help with them, or move away from that type of work, so you can move forward faster.

Against each item that you are going to develop, identify a measure of success and the steps you will take to complete them. Set targets to hit for each of those measures. After your initial update of the document, the hard part begins; staying focused on those things you wrote down and implementing them throughout the year. You should also discuss it with your manager so that they are reminded of the need to support your career development plan. This also holds you accountable to what you have written and reminds you in your day-to-day job that you have personal goals aligned to your career development. By doing this you make sure that your current job is aligned to your desired outcome at this stage of your life.

The career development plan is important to keep you focused. For many, however, if their salary is being paid, this is their main priority and causes them to get comfortable at a certain level. The challenge is that time passes very quickly. The annual cycles come around so fast. If you are not proactive about managing your own career moves, you could wake up and find you have been just comfortably stagnating in a job role and not progressing or developing at all. Enjoy the process of work and the new experiences that come with it, but also, be mindful of time spent in a job and your longer-term career goals.

It's a great idea to put at least four career development focused meetings into your personal work calendar. Then set a two-week reminder before each one. These should take place at the start of the year and then every three months. They are meetings for you and your manager to discuss your career development plan and how you are progressing against your objectives and current priorities. They should all go into your calendar, so you give your upcoming year focus. They don't need to go into your manager's calendar all at once. I would suggest that you invite your manager to each one just two weeks before each meeting, when you get the reminder. This is then close to the meeting but still gives your manager time to plan. Some managers (as surprising as it sounds) can become insecure or irritated if they feel their employees are too proactive and eager to discuss career progression, so this spaced-out approach between the meetings works well.

Keep your development plan up to date and share it at the set intervals, as per the above. If you are looking for an internal career move, you will want to have support/sponsorship from your manager and other influential stakeholders. You should always be looking at the scorecard as something that should make sense for your life and what you need to be achieving at this stage of your career.

If you ever feel that your scorecard does not align with what you want for your life or the dream you have for your career, that's a trigger for you to discuss it with your manager and see if your current role can be aligned to your career goals. If it can, great. If it can't, then you have to decide how long you want to keep going along with a role that you are not feeling connected to. It could be the time to start focusing on new target role and time period to secure it. Write down within your personal development plan for more focus and put down the necessary actions to support it.

If you don't have a career development plan, check if your organisation has a template that you can download and complete. Or you can go online and search for *career development plan template*. You will find many examples and sites to help with that plan and structure. Keep the plan updated and then make sure that it's a part of your performance review conversations, and the basis for conversations with your career mentors.

The next chapter will be looking at how you intentionally build support and a focus around you, your career and what you need for your development and progress. Your performance review conversations are not to be taken lightly. They should be your focus. You will need to make sure the managers and HR performance systems all have a good view of you as they play a significant role in your ability to progress. There are several conversations to put in place and handle well when you are working towards securing recognition for the work you have done while also trying to move forward. Let's now explore your mid-year and quarterly performance review meetings in more detail.

CHAPTER 15

PERFORMANCE REVIEW MEETINGS – BEST PRACTICE

YOUR MID-YEAR REVIEW MEETING is all about you. It is about understanding what is going well in your role and areas of development. It can feel very alarming as this is the moment you are summoned by your manager to present the evidence of how you have been performing. Don't see it in a negative light. Instead, see it as an opportunity to showcase what you are doing and the value you are bringing. To see it like that you need to actually be adding value; if not, you will dread it because the meeting will expose your poor performance. It is supposed to be a focused time to review your progress in the role, look at your achievements and your areas of development. It is a time to check how you are doing against your set objectives and to revisit your career development plan and goals.

When the 1st quarter review and mid-year review are happening, it is a good idea to have a structure for the meeting, so it stays focused on supporting your presentation and information:

1. What do you think is working well? Present your key achievements.

2. Where do you think you could/need to improve? Proactively identify areas you need to develop.

3. What ratings are you on track for? Have your manager give you an indication of this.

4. What do you need to do to get to the best rating? Ask your manager to give you an insight into your gaps and areas of improvement.

5. Review how you are progressing against your career development plan.

The last point is created by you, for you. Your manager should be interested in supporting you on this and usually is, but in some cases, managers may not be as interested in this part as it is about your goals to help you progress from where you currently are. This could ultimately be another job. Just stay focused. You should aim to cover off your main career focus/goals at that point. Raise any projects or work taking place around you that you are interested in moving into. Ask if you can support/work in that area as a development opportunity. Share any feedback that you have received from your colleagues or customers. Ask what is required for you to be considered for a promotion.

Sharing your career aspirations with your boss is important. It can sometimes happen during your mid-year review but that is mainly for assessing how you are doing in your current role, especially in your first year. It is best to wait until your year-end review to discuss your future career aspirations in more depth. This gives your manager an idea of where you want to be going and the timeframe in the back of their mind.

Now, personally, I didn't feel comfortable speaking to my manager about how I wanted to progress during the early part of my career. First of all, I didn't know what my options were, and I also didn't want my manager to start thinking I wanted to leave. I had to deal with a personal fear that once in a job, you were not *allowed* to talk about wanting to move on or gain other experiences.

Take one thing home with you: it is your right to move on and progress. From your manager's perspective, they will just want an easy life. Promotion to another team or moving on into another business is good for you but it means leaving them with a gap in their team and needing to hire a replacement. Managers can be self-interested, so you have to keep your eyes on your future and push for opportunities.

Talking about money

This is always awkward and is best raised when you have been in the role for at least a year and have a series of successes that you have delivered. In such a case, you can demonstrate that you have provided more value than was expected on your job description, that you are managing more responsibilities, and that it is reasonable to ask to receive more reward.

Caution: if you are just doing your normal job but feel that you should receive more money, unless you can prove that you are being significantly underpaid, if you have delivered nothing spectacular outside the usual expectations, a pay rise outside of the normal range, is unlikely. When you accept a job at a particular pay and benefits level that is agreed and locked in for the role, any additional annual salary increase or bonus remains at the discretion of the organisation. The final stage interviews are the best place to negotiate for what you would be happy with in terms of salary for the role. If you are doing your normal job that you agreed to, but think you should be paid more, the wisest approach is to see if you can find a similar role elsewhere that pays more and send off a job application.

You need to have a good case to justify your request for a salary increase. The most appropriate situation for the conversation would be at one of your performance meetings. In terms of approach, first share the examples that demonstrate how you are smashing your objectives, making an impact, delivering quality, and receiving good feedback from those you work with and customers. Then confirm with your manager that you are on track against your objectives and in line for a very strong performance and behavioural rating. If that is all positive, then you can ask for a pay increase. If you do not have your performance and deliverables in a very positive and impactful state, just forget about having the conversation.

If your manager agrees that you are doing above and beyond, then it is time to flip the conversation to discuss a pay rise. Say that you are adding significantly more value than you were initially hired to do and that you would like this to be reflected in your remuneration. You should receive an increase that brings your salary in line with your sustained level of high performance. Those statements should help to get the conversation going. Just remember it can feel a bit awkward, like, "how dare I be asking for this?" Perhaps that is just me, but when you have a strong case and you know your output speaks for itself, learn to be okay with raising the salary increase conversation and be bold. Ask your manager directly about how they will be recognising your expanded contribution financially.

I cannot guarantee the outcome, but I know that approach will give you a fighting chance for success. Be prepared to negotiate. If it goes negatively - an "absolutely not" situation - don't be disheartened or allow yourself to be frustrated. Just carry on with your work, keeping the atmosphere normal. Start exploring options around you because that is an indication you are exceeding expectations and the manager's response indicates you are being undervalued. As mentioned before, typically 18 months to 2 years in role, is a good point to look at new opportunities and having related conversations, as the lead time before a new role happens can take several months. 18 months to 2 years is a guide but it can, of course, be longer or shorter, there is no set rule on this.

Handling negative feedback and criticism

Now during your performance review, because it is about you, it can get quite sensitive very quickly. Nobody likes criticism. It is even more difficult when that is happening in a face-to-face situation. Your manager may mention things they think you need to improve in terms of your performance. These may be things you don't consider as serious or points that you just outright disagree with. Criticism is unpleasant and if the comments come as a surprise to you, it can quickly trigger frustration and you may immediately want to rebuff and defend yourself. The rule at work: never get pushed to the point of losing your temper and having an outburst.

In your performance review, do not get into an argument when you disagree. Know in advance that criticism bruises the ego, and then decide not to get provoked but to obtain the information you need, to address the issues your manager is raising. The sudden urge to refute what is being said and argue your case is likely to come out as defensive and with a raised voice. In defending yourself, speaking with energy and passion can come across as forceful, aggressive in tone and unprofessional. If you can't have a calm measured discussion about the negative feedback to reach a conclusion, it is best to restrain yourself and to take note of what is being said. If you don't accept it, say "Thanks for the feedback. I disagree but would like to take a day or two to reflect on what you have raised, and it would be good to then discuss it further."

You need to protect your brand and not give managers any ammunition against you. Keep calm. Breathe. Learn from what they have said. By hearing it, you can work on it. Even if you don't agree, you can further manage your actions to make sure they have no opportunity to associate you with negative feedback. Handling negative feedback and criticism is an area where many fail. Tread very carefully, especially when you are triggered. Just listen to what is being said, breathe deeply and respond calmly.

Summary of questions and checklists:

Regular career development meetings – every 6 to 12 weeks

1. Review and reconfirm your priorities.
2. How would you say I'm doing?
3. What are my strengths?
4. What are my areas for development?

Mid-year reviews – usually July / August but can vary, so whenever your company is at their mid-year point.

1. Share your views on what is working well. Ask your manager to share their views on you, too.
2. Share what could be improved or any issues.
3. Ask - What current rating level would you say I'm working at?
4. Get that information from your manager and the reasons why.
5. State the rating you are targeting and ask for their steer on how you attain that in your role.
6. Set yourself targets and goals for your performance.
7. The actions are then down to you to achieve.

End of year review – again, usually Nov – Jan but can vary, so whenever your company had their year-end.

Ask the above questions plus:

1. What would be the natural progression from this role?
2. What would I have to be demonstrating to get there?
3. Who would be good to meet in this area you mentioned?
4. Could you introduce me to them or somebody in that team?

> **Wisdom nugget:**
>
> *When it comes to feedback, just listen. If it is negative, don't react to defend yourself. Instead listen and take away any new information that will help you to be better if you change, implement, or improve things. Discard anything that is attacking or biased.*

Now the in next section, we will look at those follow-up actions in more detail. There is so much involved in moving roles, especially internally. It requires, timing – how long you have been in your role, your performance ratings, the relationships that you have internally, the information you have gathered about the actual area and, ultimately, how well you have prepared yourself for the role. The next few chapters focus on what you need to work on, how you prepare for promotion, your mind-set for your interview and internal conversations prep. Get ready to take notes!

CHAPTER 16

INTERNAL PROMOTIONS AND JOB MOVES

PROMOTIONS AND JOB MOVES, even at the same level, become more and more competitive the further up they occur within an organisation. As more people have the skills and experience, more want higher pay, seniority and responsibility, but the number of available roles at higher levels gets smaller and there is more competition. At the start of your career, the objective should be more about gaining as much experience as you can, rather than a preoccupation with the salary, especially in the first few years. That is a time when you are new to the working environment. There is so much to learn, and it is critical to strengthen yourself and build competence with a range of core skills that will enable you to increase the value you can bring to new roles and drive the potential amount you can ask for in return.

Like in the *Bossing It* case study, my colleague knew what value he could bring. It was evident in the job he was doing. He could demonstrate his experiences from a few of his previous roles, and he was clear, confident, and sure when presenting his case to ask for what he wanted. As you read, he rapidly secured a pay rise and promotion.

Promotions can sometimes happen suddenly, for example, if someone leaves unexpectedly and you have been doing a similar role and are the nearest to fill the gap. This is great but less common and there is no indication of when that could be. The sideways move is a different situation. The new role will be at the level you currently are at but will offer you different experiences and skills that you are interested in learning or keen to develop. There are some instances when there is more pressure to make a sideways move; for example, your work area being under threat of redundancies, or being closed down completely. In this case, don't just wait and hope you will escape the corporate axe swinging. It is wiser to start looking for a move out of your current 'at risk' team and into a more stable area so you can remain safe and employed.

At the performance review meeting, the usual approach to set up the promotion or job mover conversation is similar to that of the pay rise - discuss all that you have been doing and how much more you are delivering to add extra value to your team and ultimately the organisation. It's then a good idea to talk about having your role formally upgraded to a higher level to reflect all you are contributing, and for your salary to be increased as a reward for the extra effort and value that the organisation is receiving from your increased contribution. A key part of a manager's role is to develop and progress you as well as to benefit from the value you provide through your job. Managers should be having these conversations and be committed to helping you learn and experience all you can in your role and then prepare and support you to move to a new and better position. That is what a good manager does, but not all managers may be that supportive. Some managers may prefer you to stay with the organisation or even within the team, but that decision should not be up to them. It is up to you. If you feel you have reached the extent of what you can do in your role and there are no options to progress, or after months of real effort in a role, you discover that it is not a good fit for your skillset and strengths, you can search for new jobs and apply. You are free to look for other opportunities – you have choices.

Managers sometimes proactively recognise increased performance and readiness for a move upwards and approve the budget to offer a promotion and or pay rise, but this is less common. The usual scenario is one where the employee will be the one to raise the conversation. Organisations rarely just decide to give away extra money if they don't have to. They will happily just receive the profit from your increased effort that they receive for the same price - your salary, especially when you are willing to do the extra work, as my example shared in the first chapter highlighted.

In the case of a promotion, you need to make a clear and confident request for a new title to recognise the increase in your responsibilities and remit that you have demonstrated. Explain that you have an increased level of responsibility and are working on areas that are strategic for the business. When you've been delivering significantly above your job band over a sustained period, usually six months, it is the trigger for this promotion conversation. Your good performance becomes the basis for the conversation about the promotion and salary increase.

There are some cases where a promotion can be given without a pay rise – a sub-optimal scenario, as it means more responsibility and a new title, but no additional pay as a reward for the extra work or value that you are giving to the organisation. Where is your benefit for all of that? Sometimes people accept this situation in return for greater visibility and an opportunity to demonstrate what they can do in the hope of getting a pay rise in the future. It's a risky strategy as the manager who promised the future pay increase may leave before it happens, or they may later say the budgets can't support the pay increase, or just casually forget. You are then left in the sucker position.

Start the promotion conversations 6 to 12 months in advance and follow up to gain more commitments. Make sure you are in pole-position once a role becomes available or the promotion conversations start. You should have in mind a target for when you want the move to happen and have in mind when the deadline for the key decision is required. It's like a personal project where you have a target date and work backwards from that – outlining the actions and decision that need to be hit. As long as you are focused on doing your part and continue to work in a structured way, building successes under your belt, you should be in a good position and your manager should be able to share what is possible for you from their perspective.

At least four months before your target good news date, request confirmation about the status of the new responsibilities, new role or promotion discussions that you have been progressing. If possible, ask for it to be confirmed in writing. If, however, you are not receiving positive assurance, or your manager is uncertain about what is possible concerning expanding your opportunity or promotion, and not willing to make any commitments, then your concrete options are looking for opportunities outside your immediate area, internally within your company, or externally.

Managers may start to make commitments about a promotion or salary increase or offer you some extra development opportunity. It is easy for this to sound promising and to make you happy, but from my experience, nothing materialises if it is not written down and followed by actions. I would say, don't just blindly believe and assume it will happen. You will need to follow-up and carefully monitor the situation to make sure it is moving in your favour and that what was promised becomes a reality. If nothing fruitful materialises, at least you will know you had mentioned your interest in growing and progressing. You can then think about what area of interest you want to develop, and start exploring what is available internally, or externally if you are interested in opportunities outside your current organisation. In a large organisation, there may also be the possibility to experience new countries or assignments while still in your role, before deciding to make a move.

Secondments and Short-term assignments

Secondments or *short-term assignments* (STAs) are opportunities within your current job to temporarily work in another team, business area or even country to gain more experience and support a business need. Your role does not formally change but you work in a different role for a period. The duration can be from two weeks, up to 2 years, with you focused on delivering a special project, or to filling a resource gap. They can be in country which involves moving to a new team for a period of time or they can be international. When they are international, your accommodation and travel are usually paid for by your organisation, and even an additional living allowance may be provided in some cases. They are not widespread but do exist in large organisations.

As secondments and STAs are temporary in nature, after a period of working in the role, where it is really enjoyed and you make strong connections, you can see if there is an opportunity to be made permanent so the job you have been doing becomes your new formal role. Sometimes STAs are offered where the business has an urgent need to fill a gap and cannot hire people. You can go for these opportunities by just saying "yes." If you are initiating the STA or secondment discussion, the best way is to ask your manager or managers in your network if there are any needs for such an assignment. There would have to be a business need and willingness for you to support the work. You then aim to clearly communicate how the STA/secondment would support your development and work to obtain your manager support and approval.

In many cases, internal moves, promotions, STAs and secondments, require planning and external support from sponsors and stakeholders connected to the role, too. Having catch-ups with relevant and influential decision-makers to express what you want and why you would be great for it, is extremely helpful. The package of your good work, great ratings and positive feedback is your foundation to build on. These decision-makers can then work in your favour behind the scenes. The promotion planning process starts by assessing - What are your next role options? What do you need to know to get your target role? Who are the stakeholders managing that role? Next steps include looking at how you can get time with them to discuss getting into that position.

Speak to your mentors or trusted colleagues about how to position yourself and your skills for those conversations. Role-play interview questions or ask them to let you know what is expected in that new role or job area. Also, find a few contacts in areas that you are targeting and have an informal conversation with them, to get deeper insights about the priorities and areas of focus. This helps you to build up your connections in that team and gain an understanding of how that area works. All of this will work together to turn you into a stronger candidate, known by the business area as being interested.

It is always good to maintain a strong and positive relationship with anyone who could potentially offer you a job role. That includes regular meetings, discussing roles and your complementary skills and experience, etc. so that if anything comes up you will be at the top of their mind. This is just making your intentions clear and keeping the relationship warm. What I would caution against is morphing into people-pleasing or attaching yourself to a manager in an excessive way and trying to use the relationship to get a promotion. It looks terrible to your peers and even if you have the skills and capability, the approach can make you lose credibility with those who work for that manager.

> **Wisdom nuggets:**
>
> - *Internally for job promotions – the story people tell about you when you aren't there is more powerful/damaging than the story you tell about yourself in an interview – personal brand.*
>
> - *We may think we are great, but we are not the decision-makers when it comes to new opportunities. Keep in mind that you influence the narrative about you by your day-to-day behaviour and your work ethic, both of which are driven by everyday actions.*
>
> - *Keep senior relationships warm but remain professional and avoid people-pleasing behaviours.*

Now most jobs will still require a CV to be presented to go through the interview process. The next chapter will deal with the best approaches for CV preparation, researching the role and getting ready for interviews.

CHAPTER 17

WINNING CV AND INTERVIEW PREP

A DEAR JOB BUDDY ADVISED ME – be able to tell your story. How do your previous roles link to where you are going? How can you let your potential employer know that you have ticked the boxes they are looking for? Make sure your career journey makes sense to a potential employer, in relation to the opportunity that you want them to offer you. Ahead of an interview spend time focusing on this. Think about this story and then imagine you are asked the question, "Tell me about your career journey so far." Practise explaining your career overview in a way that summarises your relevant experience in line with what the new job requires.

Position yourself with a great CV

Your CV is often your first opportunity to present your personal brand. It is an opportunity for a potential employer to get to know you. Your CV should give an overview of you, your experience and an indication of what you are capable of. Leave your contact details right at the top and then follow with a short summary about you. Your overall experience and what you are looking for in a maximum of 100 words.

Education and qualifications are often included: some prefer them at the beginning and others share at the end. When you are starting out and possible have less working experience education is fine to follow the introduction.

Next would be your work experience and previous jobs. Read up on the required skills for the job that you are seeking or the area that you want to get in to. Make sure that you tailor your experiences and the jobs that you include so that you show the CV reviewer that your experience is aligned to the required experience for the role you are applying for.

For each of the roles you include, present you actual responsibilities and a few stand out achievements that you delivered during the role. Make sure you share what you did rather than what your team did. If you do any voluntary work or have side hustles, your own personal work or projects, include them if they demonstrate relevant capabilities for the role you are seeking. Just ensure that you clearly explain that this work is done outside your working hours.

Your CV should give an overview of you and should be concise and summarised, highlighting your strengths and suitability for the job you are applying for. Keep your CV focused to one page if you are starting your career journey from school, and if you have had 2-5 years + experience you should aim to be as concise as possible to achieve a CV on 2 pages max. After you have included your job roles and relevant qualifications, include a line about hobbies and interests outside of work to give your potential employer a view of who you are. Any additional languages, volunteering, travel, adventure, food and music-related interests all work well.

Knowing your worth is important and making sure you effectively put it across will make your CV stand out. Regularly update your CV and make sure you share what your core responsibilities are, including any key achievements you have had. Keeping your LinkedIn profile up to date is important as many people will use it to do a first screening of you before progressing your application. Make sure your social media will not damage you because of your comments or associations. If you don't want to limit how much you post, it is best to set your personal social media accounts to private. A colleague once said "Selling yourself is hard but when it comes to a job, you have to be your best salesperson."

Do detailed research into any role you are going for. Understand what will be required of you. Reach out to contacts who work in that area. You can find them on your company's internal systems, or if the role is external you can find them on LinkedIn. Just be discreet and say, "I'm interested in finding out more about your business area and would like to connect to have a conversation." That is usually enough. See if you can find out what the company's strategic priorities are. Study the job description in detail and make sure that your CV, the main experiences and examples that you want to share, are in line with that new role. Your experiences don't only have to come from your current job. Your relevant experiences can come from former jobs and even from your personal life and hobbies. Focus yourself on the job and share only what is relevant for supporting your case as a great candidate.

Keep your eye on your market value. Search online to get an idea of the salary for the role and also talk to colleagues or recruiters to give you a sense of what the salary range is. It may vary based on experience, but you will have a much better idea of what you should expect. The update of your CV and seeing all that you have accomplished laid out can give you a real confidence boost, especially if you have been receiving a lower salary than the industry average for a prolonged amount of time.

In an interview scenario, that first date kind of shyness does not work. Be assertive and clearly let them know you are interested. Be explicit about what you want. The weakest position is being vague, especially when you are before the key decision-maker. They are not a career advisor; they are the person who will decide to hire you or not. The Bible says, "A double-minded man is unstable in all his ways." That is how you will come across when you are unsure of yourself. Ask questions during the interview, using it as an opportunity to learn more about the culture, the team and the role. Trial all the interview scenarios with a friend, mentor or trusted person before you enter the actual job interview, promotion or salary increase conversation.

This practice preparation is really important because often, these conversations can feel really awkward and uncomfortable, they do take a while to get used to. Practice helps you to overcome those feelings and be bold. It's even hard for people who do have experience, but it just has to be done. Step into a new character and role-play saying what you want, until you feel you are sure of yourself and can come across confidently (but not arrogantly).

As discussed in the *Bossing It* case study, rather than approaching a job from a place of desperation and need, imagine offering your skills from your abundance of talent. To really bring it home, keep in your mind - *They need you!* Your skills, intelligence, experience and energy are what they need to solve their problems. The successful candidate meets their need. If that is you, in return, you should expect a certain level of salary and benefit in return. Know your value and what you have to offer. In an interview situation, as much as they are deciding on you, you are also deciding on them. Does the role offer you the potential to grow, develop and contribute your value?

When you accept a new role, you should enter a mutually beneficial partnership and agreement. This may seem like a completely different way to look at a job interview situation, but I had to wake up to that and embrace it. *You need me* is the strongest mental approach for positioning yourself for a new job. That short statement in your mind, helps you remember your value and capabilities. As much as you may want the job, if you are the right candidate, you are a solution that will contribute great value. They need you. You therefore have the right to negotiate for the salary you require. Research the market rate by simply googling. Companies are often trying to get you to agree to a certain salary, so if a salary that is less than expected is offered be prepared to negotiate. Just approach with confidence, not arrogance and have clarity on the value you possess. Negotiate for what you expect from your abundance of skill, talent and experience and citing the value that will deliver. If successful, great! At the very least you raise what you expect and build the case for more.

Job applications online

Job applications online should never be all you rely on. As a sensible guesstimate, you have about a 30-40% chance for success when you arc going in cold and unknown by anybody connected to the role being offered. These are a few of the reasons why:

- You are unknown – employers often have preferred candidates and reach out to people in their own network that they think could do the job, as happened to me at the start of my career and several times since.

- You will have to perform well in the interview as well as build rapport at the same time.

- You don't have the context that comes from working within that team or area.

- Your background research and experience will need to be presented clearly within the interview and if possible before you get into the interview situation, if you are connected to somebody who works within the company, who even knows the hiring manager, ask them to give you a recommendation for the role. This will significantly help your application and as they share their experience of you.

If you demonstrate to interviewers that you meet the criteria there is nothing that stops them from taking a chance on you rather than internal hires. It happens all the time so go for it!

Following these actions on a hunt for a new opportunity will likely present that new job opportunity. An important thing to reiterate for anyone who may have been like me in chapter one – there is nothing wrong with receiving a new opportunity through someone directly offering you a new job, or you actively looking for a new opportunity. You are allowed to move on, and it can be triggered in many ways!

It is normal and a good thing to have new job opportunities. It gives you the chance to develop and take on more responsibility as you desire. The more you progress, the more you gain new skills, experience and confidence. That's a constant journey. Organisations also expect that you will be leaving your existing job at some point - it's not disloyal. Just a part of your career development.

A few practical things to do to increase your success in online applications:

1. **Proofread your CV.** This might sound basic but so many CVs fall at the first hurdle because of typos. Read, read and read your CV again – then ask a friend, family member or colleague to check it, too.

2. **Present your CV clearly.** Again, this might sound basic but recruiters only have a short time to read each applicant's CV. Make their job easier by presenting information clearly

and concisely. There are lots of CV templates, examples and writing resources freely available on the internet too.

3. **Keep it honest!** Avoid the temptation to exaggerate your experience. You can create long-term damage to your reputation if you are found out. The skills, knowledge, and experiences that you already have are sufficient in themselves, so just focus on what you've achieved so far.

The next chapter will be looking at the dos and don'ts in terms of meetings. These two fundamental elements of the workplace experience are too often handled very casually. Yet so much about your professionalism and awareness of the way things operate is communicated through your meeting conduct.

PART FIVE

THE DOs AND DON'Ts

Please take note

CHAPTER 18

MEETINGS – DOs AND DON'Ts

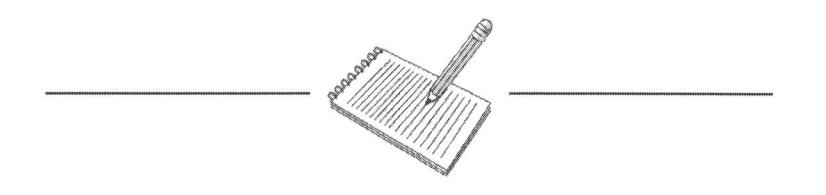

IN THE EARLY PART OF MY CAREER, I would share my opinions freely in whatever setting I was in. In many cases it was okay but in some cases, to my surprise there was an adverse reaction. That resulted in me rapidly learning after some embarrassing and awkward moments, that in some cases, I needed to do some pre-work and check with managers or other key stakeholders before sharing or sending a response. In all instances, the pre-work, caution and preparation, made a huge difference and always made show up more confidently and in control.

Meeting conduct – guidance and advice

Meetings are one of the most common activities in the corporate world. Doing the basics will build a strong foundation for the more complex aspects that surround meetings:

- Be punctual – it's a given. If you are running late send apologies in advance.

- Be prepared – do the pre-reading, and if you are presenting, prepare well, to deliver well.

- Have an agenda – if you are running a meeting, keep the focus on the key items to discuss.

- Stick to time – set out how long you will need for each of the agenda items.

- Confirm actions and who is responsible – after discussion, there needs to be agreements and people taking responsibility for the work to be done. Otherwise, the meeting was a waste of time.

- Agree when you will review – action, owners and deadlines for delivery – and the next meeting date.

- Send meeting notes/minutes after meeting – confirm the outcomes and hold all accountable.

Effective note taking – write down the decisions that were agreed and the new plan or approach that was agreed. That will be your summary of the meeting outcome. Then whatever needs to be done is an *action*. An *action* is a task that was raised in the meeting and needs to be completed before you meet again. Logging the actions is just making a list of the actions. Each time they come up during the meeting, write an A and circle it, then write out the action and put the name of the person who is to deliver it and the date it will be due. You can then see all the circled A's and easily just write them into an email.

In the early part of your career, you can often find yourself in a meeting where you may be the most junior person there. It is best to listen first, pick up how people are phrasing their questions and how they are landing their points. You can still share your ideas or questions; just don't ramble and get straight to the point and if possible, write down the question in advance and practise saying it a few times, in order to land solid points.

For larger meetings that give you access to managers outside of your team, asking a question in the meeting is a good way to build an initial connection. Once the meeting is over, you can then follow-up by sending an email thanking them for their response and sharing your further ideas or asking for a catch-up. That connection could then be the start of a new mentoring or sponsorship relationship, so be clear on exactly why you want to follow-up.

In a meeting with seniors where you are in an audience, if something comes up that you don't agree with, that public forum is not the place for you to challenge or, worse, have an argument or show defiance. Please, never start an argument or try and win one in a public meeting setting. Your brand is on the line, your professionalism is on the line, and there are so many other ways you can handle it. A knee jerk outburst rather than exercising self-control can be very costly! If you must, set a time after the meeting to discuss. This is always better as you will feel calmer and can land your points more objectively, without added emotion. At most say, "I have a different viewpoint. We could consider xxx, but I'm happy to take that offline and have a separate conversation." This is a professional and respectable way to disagree.

There should never be an argument at work especially not in public. In a meeting, if there is already team tension and a point of direct address is raised against you, control yourself. It is so easy for one to be frustrated and fall into the trap of being called aggressive when you express your point directly and with passion. It is common for people to be called unprofessional or emotional, so anticipate this and decide that you will conduct yourself in a measured and professional way, even when you are frustrated. The only exception is when the manager has frankly said, "Team, let's deal with this now. I want to hear all the views laid out on the table and I want you to be honest." This suggests that they are willing to hear honest feedback. But rather than just blurting out exactly how you are feeling, still handle this with professionalism.

Now in addition to this kind of planning and pre-empting, I also began to observe closely and learn the dos and don'ts when it came to meetings. Hopefully, the insights will help you on your journey.

For the larger meetings, where you need to get to a specific outcome, it is beneficial to plan ahead for the outcome that you want to see happen before the meeting. Explain to different attendees what you want to see happen and share your desired outcome, so you talk it all through and agree to it *before* the deciding meeting. This was so strange to me at first but when I saw the amount of work that went into connecting with decision-makers ahead of a meeting to share views or a position and gain agreement or support, I knew I needed to wake up.

My most interesting discovery when it came to large meetings was that the decision-makers could be warmed up to the outcome I hoped for beforehand, so that when the meeting actually took place, it was just a formality. The desired outcome was already cooking. That applied to business decisions that needed to be made as well as putting yourself forward for a new opportunity. Don't wait until the deciding meeting to present your desire. Start warming decision-makers up, even before the event. This is just one of many subtle things that make the difference between someone who shows up woke to all this and someone who comes across as naïve and asleep.

Finally, minor negative things done over time become major things. For the rest of these meetings, "don'ts" should be obvious, but I will just share to fully expose them and serve as a reminder.

Avoid lateness as far as possible. Frequently checking your phone during a meeting can be seen as rude and just communicates that you are distracted. Loudly chewing gum is a no-no, please. Eating in a meeting should also be avoided, unless it is a lunch meeting, or the meeting is happening virtually and you are just listening in. In the virtual setting, switch your camera off and go on mute before eating. Sharing your point should be done politely. Talking over someone, interrupting, not listening or shouting – all come across as unprofessional and create a negative impression of you. Be patient and be mindful of how you share your point. Finally, if you need to take a call, rather than trying to quietly have the phone discussion in the meeting, excuse yourself or go on mute.

Even more than meetings, emails play a huge role in communicating and sharing of ideas in the workplace. Though they are very familiar to most of us, they still can cause issues if not delivered optimally or sent with care. In the next chapter we look at emails in more detail.

CHAPTER 19

EMAILS – DOs AND DON'Ts

EMAILS ARE THE MOST COMMON and easy form of communication in the workplace, but they can also be a potential minefield and you need to tread carefully. Sending an email isn't just a method of communication when you are doing so within the workplace; there can be a lot of complexity or politics involved. Paying close attention to who is receiving it and who is copied on the email is really important. Even if constant emailing is a requirement of your job, still be intentional and tread with care. In this chapter, we will cover the basics and some wider considerations to keep in mind, which will keep you in the best practice zone and protect how you are perceived when it comes to your emails.

Recap of the basics *– I share these not to patronise, but more as a gentle reminder of the main things.*

Start and close your emails with "Hi xxx," and end with "Kind regards, xxx." I say this because we are in the social media age where messages are more and more casually sent. I have been guilty of just whizzing over my one-sentence reply without even adding my work signature. When I then receive a reply and see someone has taken the time to structure it properly, I definitely feel the internal check that I could have just made that small change to keep it professional. Build your brand.

Always check who you are sending the email "To" and who needs to be "cc." If the message needs to be forwarded, think about it. Does the recipient need to see all the background email part? Or only the new top part. If they don't need to see all the history, make sure that you delete the bottom part that is not relevant for them, or that they should not be seeing. Such a mistake could be embarrassing at the least, and career-altering at worst, especially if you forward information that is sensitive or restricted, that the recipient should not have access to.

When deciding to email people who are above your manager's level - be careful. There is nothing necessarily wrong with it, but it is so easy to just copy someone into an email. You need to also think to yourself, "In real life, would I naturally walk up to that person and share this message? Or would I have spoken to someone closer to me for advice first? Or would I have contacted someone who works for them to resolve my query rather than bothering them?" Think about your role relative to a colleague's role and whether your email will be stepping outside the normal structure.

If you are copied on an email with other managers, or with your manager on copy too, ask yourself this question: "Has your manager given you responsibility in this area? Is it something that has been delegated to you to deal with on their behalf?" or "Is it something your manager is responsible for and you are included as an FYI?" Unless you have been asked to intervene, or you have responsibility for the specific query being raised, in large multi-level emails like that, it is always better to check with your manager before responding.

Often, we may want to respond to help or be proactive, but managers frequently prefer to control what message is going to their seniors, so in group emails that include your manager and other stakeholders – wait. Let your manager respond unless you are fully delegated the responsibility and actually have the answer. This creates more order than just launching out in response, which could then lead to many more open questions that your manager ultimately has to answer and may not be expecting or be prepared for. Your "helpful" interjection could end up making them look like they aren't in control. These are the kind of things you have to consider, especially within very large organisations. There is a considered approach which will ultimately protect you, or a naïve approach which will expose you and can be quite costly. Be wise.

With emails that need to outline or present a lot of information, at the start, give your recipient an overview of what the email is about and what you need from them – include a two-line summary, a clear request/ask and a deadline for response. "1. This email contains xxx, 2. Please review and confirm xxx / Please review and select xxx, 3. and reply by xxx." For detailed subjects that need to be shared via email, this approach helps the reader understand upfront what is expected from them and by when. Then you will still need to focus on the body of the email being as concise as possible. Conclude with a reminder of the main ask and the deadline for response.

Emails can be a quick way to send a lot of information immediately, and where a person is unavailable on the phone or in person, it provides that information for them to pick up at their convenience. Emails are also key for documenting activity and can be used to confirm that managers have been made aware of something because they are copied on an email that was sent. It acts as the proof so they cannot really say they were not aware of something that is later escalated. This highlights the point that our email box is a corporate communication exchange, and we are expected to use it to consume and communicate business-critical information.

If you need to send an email that requires real care, check in with your manager and make sure they have reviewed it with you and approved it to go out, especially with other teams or senior colleagues. As you develop more, you may lean less on your manager, but they are there to shield you and the team from negative impact as far as possible so align with them on more complex issues, a wider audience or senior emails. This action highlights your understanding of the workplace sensitivities, demonstrating your ability to act responsibly, avoid risk and handle sensitive messages and situations - all great for your brand and demonstrating a professional approach.

If you're annoyed or frustrated, or there is an issue, a very wise woman once said to me, "Before sending an email – pause and think: if this email landed in anybody's inbox and they read it, how would it make you look? Would you come away from that looking good or bad?" This is a very important consideration and sometimes tone and feeling can come through even if the words look professional. So be mindful of that.

You really are the most responsible person for protecting your brand. You should never come across as arrogant, commanding, argumentative or condescending. Always be professional, concise and solution focused. Never put sensitive intentions in an email - conversations about promotion, increasing your responsibilities, a pay increase or discussing personal business issues. Always have such conversations in a meeting, over the phone or in person.

Similarly, never send anything that could damage you if it were publicly shared - inappropriate jokes, negativity towards any colleague, private and confidential information that was discussed with you in confidence, negative sentiments about your organisation, client or other information that the recipient should not have access to. Once your email is sent - it is sent. Things can be copied and pasted easily – what you thought was just a casual back and forth between two trusted parties can be used as evidence against you in the future. Just remember that you are attached to anything that you write and send, regardless of where it goes or how long ago it was sent, the context, or any other type of reasoning. As you have sent it, you own it. Be wise.

If sending emails to your team, usually it's okay to send back and forth - but it's good to try and talk to people or conclude what you need in a few exchanges. Now if you are emailing a colleague who is senior to you, your manager's level or above, tread with more care. This is where reading over your emails is even more important, to make sure you remove all unnecessary information, any possible mistakes, and keep it as short and focused as possible. Peer review is also helpful, especially when the email is addressing, or is part of, a more complex issue. Another thing to bear in mind is, your level/grade. You may not be privy to the wider activity happening and you also may not be aware of people who have been given different responsibilities for finding solutions, because you newly entered the conversation.

There is no such thing as a dumb question, but it's more about whether it was something that you needed to put into an email or could have answered by just picking up the phone. Avoid emails about very simple matters that copy in loads of people, and avoid including senior managers without a real need for doing so. It makes you look like you aren't aware of other peoples' time and priorities - it can make you look very inexperienced and unprofessional.

Every email requires reading and a response and is, therefore, a distraction, just like a phone call. For the other person, they all become urgent, though potentially "Not Important," as we saw within the Eisenhower matrix prioritisation model. To avoid wasting your recipient's time, assess if what you are sending or calling about is a necessary distraction. Then aim to get straight to the point. Don't rush. Pause before you send and do a check over what you have written to make sure it is fine. Re-read longer emails to remove unnecessary information or waffle for clarity.

By pausing and checking before you send you will ensure that very common mistakes are avoided. Final things to check before you press send. Have you:

- completed a spell check and read through to see that it makes sense?
- included the attachment needed with the message?
- read the messages in the email chain before, so you don't end up asking a question that has already been answered?
- checked the right people and addresses are copied in?
- removed any background text that should not be forwarded on, if applicable?
- made sure your email is as concise as possible with a clear ask?
- confirmed that you are in place to answer? (group senior emails, not your team or one-to-ones)

> **Wisdom nuggets:**
>
> - *Sending times - unless it is critically important, avoid sending emails around or after 5pm on Friday evening. The weekend has begun, and you risk your email being missed. Better to send your emails during the day and within the working week.*
> - *Read your emails, flag important ones, clear all spam mail and minimise non-business-related communication, to make sure you see the most important information.*

The moral of this chapter: be intentional about how you manage your emails. It requires you to be present to the process of emailing and is something so easy to execute that important considerations are easily overlooked, which can create issues or costly mistakes.

CHAPTER 20

WORK RELATIONSHIPS - THE ESSENTIALS

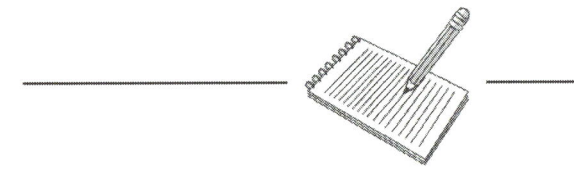

I HAVE SHARED A LOT ON THE DIFFERENT PEOPLE you meet along your career journey through the workplace – colleagues of many types; direct managers, sponsors, mentors, teammates, other managers, colleagues who are helpers, colleagues who are possibly in competition. There are so many workplace relationships, so aim to protect how you are viewed, by carefully managing how you interact with your colleagues. It's really important. Do your best to ensure that you show up positively throughout your career.

No one of us is perfect but remember that people will always be talking and not always with you. What are they saying *about* you? That will be based on who you are when you think nobody is watching. That is why it is so important to catch yourself quickly when you are coasting and not working at your best. As far as possible avoid being negative. Firmly addressing an issue or raising a problem isn't being negative. Negativity is more related to the attitude that goes with your actions or words.

To avoid the issues raised in the last chapter on HR procedures, maintain a positive and professional relationship with your managers as well as your peers as far as possible. Think past this moment and be intentional about forming a real connection with people you click with. It could be for friendship, career progress, guidance, reference or someone who offers you an opportunity to partner or collaborate with them. The possibilities are endless. Make time to go for coffee, to go for drinks, ask about family and friends, work, etc. Make a note of what you discussed and make sure you follow-up on anything you agreed. By so doing, you come across as credible and enhance your brand/image.

Tim Sanders, the bestselling author, once said that "your network is your net-worth." But that can only happen if you activate your relationships. Remember people will only put you forward for new jobs or introduce you to people looking for someone to hire if they can trust that you will not embarrass them by doing a bad job if you get the role. A sponsor, mentor, former boss or family friend who puts you forward for something is attaching their reputation to the referral. You will need to commit to doing a good job to make them look good. Regardless of how great you are to be around, if you ask for support from them for a job, the question in a manager's mind will always be – can you deliver? Friendship and getting along are good but reputations are at risk as it will always be about your ability to deliver what is required. Always remember to be visible for adding value and delivering quality work on time.

You can get attached to colleagues and managers who you really get along with, and it can be very sad to see them move on. What I have noticed is that it is quite challenging to stay in touch after someone goes. You might even have been super close but when they move on, you never see each other again. Now colleagues you click with could also become part of your wider network if you intentionally maintain contact when they leave, and it is important to do so to avoid losing potentially valuable links. At the very least connect on LinkedIn; it's a great way to at least keep the virtual connection and stay up to date on their progress.

At the start of careers, as I alluded to in Chapter 1, if a manager has greatly inspired you or been so good to you, maybe given you your first real job or major opportunity, emotional attachment can occur. It can also happen with first organisations, where you have had a great experience. When another opportunity comes up, this emotional connection can make it difficult to leave. You may feel that the company has invested time and resources into you and as we have seen previously, feelings of disloyalty, betrayal or ungratefulness may arise because of the new possibility of you moving on to a new role internally, or externally.

Emotional ties with an organisation or team can be deeply rooted and hard to spot but they are sentiments that cause you to feel more connected, and possibly less willing to move or progress your career when there are other opportunities. At all times you should be focused on doing what is right for you. As your career develops, it becomes clear that to progress you need to have a focus and be sure of what you want and where you need to go. It is business at the end of the day. Wonderful that you can feel so attached but don't lose your perspective. Get over any feelings of dependence on a manager or abandonment if a manager leaves. Even if you are friends or have a good relationship, remember that you have a commitment to yourself and your life, to progress and accomplish everything that you have the potential to achieve. Jobs in organisations are also not guaranteed. Employers also face tough decisions and from time to time, have to make the people they like redundant.

Understandably, the closeness of some relationships at work is born out of a need for survival or support in that moment. If that is the case and a detachment happens for some reason, don't mourn it. Accept it as a great working relationship for a season. If the relationship evolves and you can maintain it, it is a great addition to your wider professional network and could even become a friendship. If your colleague doesn't want to stay in touch after they have moved on, be okay with that. Don't ever force things.

A note of caution for single people: work can be a natural place to meet a suitable partner but relationships at work can also make things complicated, so be careful. I strongly caution against getting romantically involved with your manager or anyone in the same team or business area as you. There is too much potential for your personal business to be exposed and a conflict of interest to arise. If you do develop a romantic relationship at work, make sure you review the company policies. Some company policies will require you to disclose your relationship early on and others prohibit a relationship of there is a line manager connection. I have known some couples in this situation and they have agreed that one of them would move to a different team or company to enable their relationships to survive and thrive. Staying in the team would have caused too much conflict but some workplace distance and confirming a sensible approach to protect your privacy and maintain professionalism can be enough for workplace relationships to flourish.

Now, the following is a strong NO – developing unprofessionally close relationships with a colleague who is married or in a relationship. Colleagues may be going through personal challenges at home and using work as an escape. Working later, spending more time socialising with colleagues. Nothing wrong with that but just be mindful when there is any spark of an attraction. Intense projects, working late, long chats and travelling home together are all situations that can allow for emotions to build over time. Let the ring or knowledge of a partner be a barrier to progressing beyond the professional point with any colleague that is already committed to another person. My advice: don't even entertain the temptation.

Build the most amazing career story for your life. If you are offered a job somewhere else as we previously discussed, this is a great thing. Not betrayal. It just means somebody has recognized your talent and wants to give you a new opportunity. Weigh up the new offer against the current role you are in and the opportunities around you. Where could you have the most opportunity to be the best version of you in the next three years?

It is always best to have any commitments to you in writing – new job, new salary. The contract is what formally confirms it is taking place. If you receive promises, they are just words and goodwill, which can change. Take time out to get real clarity on the best decision for you. Progress can happen where you are in your team and within your organisation. It can also happen by leaving one organisation for another, or starting one yourself.

When you move on, leave on a good note as far as possible and share your details for colleagues to stay in touch with you. For those work relationships with managers or colleagues that you really get on with, commit to nurturing those relationships and connections after you leave. Set up periodic catch-ups or lunches, meet up for drinks, invite them to events, or share relevant information that would be of interest to them. These are just ideas on how to keep connections alive. It requires you to be intentional and proactive to maintain them. The investment in maintaining the relationship after working together, will at minimum expand your network of professional contacts who may be able to support or assist you in future.

CHAPTER 21

LOST YOUR FOCUS? GET IT BACK!

MOMENTS CAN COME when you feel less enthusiastic about your work. It happens to everyone, but you must take control over that feeling, catch it quickly and work on targeting what specifically is making you feel less enthusiastic and less empowered. Whatever the cause is, pinpoint it and resolve it, because it only gets worse if you don't address it and can affect how you are performing in your job. Sometimes taking time away from the situation - a walk, a break, a few days off - can help you reset and recharge at the same time. Fully disconnecting and having time to rest, charge and reset can change how you're feeling. Challenging times in roles can occur. It is part of the ups and downs of work, but you can always make the most out of every situation. It does not have to go on for a prolonged period.

Shift out of that feeling as quickly as possible because if you continue feeling down about work, it can result in you becoming more negative and losing your energy and concentration. It can arise from something that has wound you up or repeatedly negative actions, but this phase cannot last long without being confronted. This is not the space you want to be in, and it can creep up on you leading to lower performance, making mistakes and/or just not being the best version of yourself. The longer you're not being your best self, the more you could become at risk of negative perception from your manager and being at risk in your role.

If there is a lack of motivation and negative feeling caused by the job itself or your manager over a prolonged period, ask yourself some key questions.

- Is the job providing me with access to the skills I need to build at this stage in my career?
- Does my working environment enable me to grow?
- Are there opportunities to develop further in my role?
- Is the job the best option available to me right now?
- Am I interested in the work I am doing?

If at least three out of five of those questions are broadly a "yes," your role will help you to develop and progress; you can't afford to waste the opportunity. Shake the feeling, focus on the positives that exist; the most basic one – that you actually have the job. Aim to make the most of it. Set yourself targets and determine to hit them. Push to get faster at getting things done. You can do it! Don't let yourself become a victim of negativity.

If all the answers are a confident "no," it would suggest you are in the wrong job - in that case, you should just make a plan. Look at your strengths and your interests and think of the jobs you want to do. For as long as you're there before you get access to a new opportunity, aim to do the best you can. Your manager will be providing a reference, and situations can also be turned around when you change your perspective and look for the positives.

Remember these key things: in the early stages of your career, you need to push to be confident in your skills and increase what you're able to do. There will be much which is new to you and just like building new muscle, it will really hurt as you push yourself to reach your goals. To achieve that new level of fitness, you have to be consistent and keep going. Just face it and remain determined to make it happen. Take the support that is available to you and find someone who will motivate you – mentor or colleague. Get to your next level.

To become a specialist requires intentional on the job learning and home study time. Unfortunately, there is no escaping it. No amount of sweet talk or interpersonal skills can cover up when you don't have the depth of understanding. Your bluffing and surface knowledge will very quickly get found out. You need to put the effort in; stick it out in roles to achieve what is possible, but this requires real work. Most times, being honest with yourself about where you have been lazy challenges you to focus and progress your development.

Here are some checks that you can do to understand why you're feeling the way you are, and actions you can take to help you get back your focus:

1. Identify what caused the feeling. If it is a piece of work you just don't like or a backlog of tasks that are draining, set a time limit to finish them and get over it. If it is a conflict with a colleague, make time to catch up and discuss it, sharing the situation and your view, hearing their feedback, and aiming to work out a solution.

2. Focus on dealing with the issue or work that is causing the negative feeling. Don't let it continue.

3. Remember who you are – What are your core skills? What gets you excited? What are you interested in? Who are you on your best day?

4. Look at what new skills/knowledge will take your work to the next level? What could you do to make your contribution or work shine? How could you make yourself/your work more valuable?

5. Make up your mind to push past the feeling. It will pass when you are determined.

6. Set targets for what needs to shift immediately!

7. Celebrate yourself when you know you have seen a breakthrough. Enjoy it!

In rare cases, you may really have tried and just cannot learn the knowledge required to shine. It just isn't a role that plays to your strengths, and your transferable skills are not strong enough to help keep you floating. I would say, give it a year to see how you progress. In such cases, see if your role can be refocused on areas where you can support and contribute more value to the team. If that is not possible or things don't improve, don't risk affecting your performance ratings by delivering mediocre work or worse, making costly mistakes. The worst thing is when you stay too long operating beneath your potential and junior people, who have strengths that fit in that role, find it easier to upskill and surpass you. Get into a space where you can shine. Speak to mentors, set a target, work as hard as possible where you are and boldly prepare yourself to create new options and opportunities to move forward.

The next chapter looks at what you can do if a mistake does occur. We all make mistakes, but some mistakes are more serious than others and they carry different consequences in the workplace. It is just best to operate responsibly to avoid them but also not to cave into thinking it is the end of the world if they occur. We now going to explore approaches to deal with mistakes and negative by-products that can arise as a result.

CHAPTER 22

MISTAKES – BOUNCING BACK

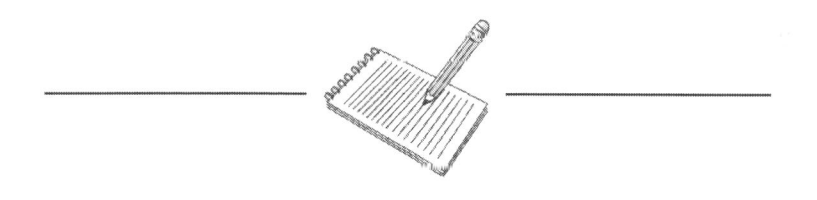

WE ALL MAKE MISTAKES. It could be sending off the wrong email, copying in people that you didn't need to. It could be sending a document that you later realise has an error on it. It could be lateness for a meeting, or even missing a key meeting. Not completing certain fields correctly on an important submission, forgetting to do the key step of a process, intruding on a situation, or saying something you regret in a meeting. No matter how bad the mistake is, someone somewhere has likely done much worse. If you make a big mistake, the best response is always to acknowledge and accept your responsibility, commit to the resolution, learn from it, and move on. Denial shifts a possible pardon into a guaranteed punishment.

In addressing the situation, keep in mind that a mistake is in the past which means you can take actions after it has happened, to limit its effect on your future. Don't let it become the biggest thing in your life or waste time wallowing in the mess. The default action is to beat yourself up about it, feel sick, stay in regret and worry, and imagine all the bad things that can happen as a result. These are all natural reactions but as you will fully know, they are not helpful. None of them can correct the issue. They only make you feel worse and keep you wasting time, feeling low and not taking action.

Commit to action planning towards a solution, and fast! Look at all the avenues to stop the problem, reduce or remove the negative impact and bring to the attention of your manager the solution you have in place. In some emergency situations, you may need to reach out to a trusted mentor or advisor for advice first, and get extra wisdom as needed to confirm the most optimal approach. But with mistakes, you should not delay introducing a solution. Don't let the issue linger unresolved. Identify who needs to be informed and engage as soon as possible, if not immediately.

The best thing to do in the case of a mistake that is minor, low risk and in your control is just update, correct and complete the fix. Show your manager that you have corrected the issue and understood and addressed the causes. Then make sure you just learn the personal lesson. Learn from that mistake and change whatever it was that caused it. Write the mistake in a notepad. This will act as a strong reminder too, so that it cannot creep up again. You will have called it out as far as possible; do not allow yourself to repeat it. If that happens, it's a sign that something you are doing is letting you down and you need to pinpoint it and decide that you will address it.

For anything that is in the more serious category such as not following conduct expectations, critical training missed, some misconduct that impacts your business, team or customers. Make sure you inform your manager. Don't try and cover it up or manage it alone. It may be that your manager and/or your colleagues will need to know so that the mistake can be resolved in the best way. This is the most responsible way to manage more serious mistakes, as they could have a wider impact. By owning up as soon as you realise what you have done, you put yourself in a better position. Covering up mistakes will result in worse outcomes when found out, so don't take that risk. Whatever happens, it will not be the end of the world. In the worst-case scenario there are always other jobs.

The solution at the time of the mistake is to acknowledge what has happened and be calm and focused. Don't waffle but get to the point. Take responsibility for your actions and share suggestions of what you want to do to fix the situation. Get agreement from your manager or peers on the best approach to a solution and get it done. Once you have worked on the solution, don't allow the playback of "How could this happen?" roam around in your brain. If it does come up, simply say to yourself, "I have done what I can do" and move on.

Be kind to yourself and forgive yourself even if the manager you share it with reacts badly. Some mistakes take a lot of work to resolve and can sometimes cause embarrassment, not just to you but also to your managers, so bad reactions can occur. They may also be under some other pressure or just be having a bad day so if there is a backlash, don't take it personally. Just remain committed to the fix, acknowledging what was done and stay focused on the solution. Don't beat yourself up about it or let anyone else beat you up about it.

Some people are negative and want to hold grudges against people and can also be unforgiving. Following a mistake, once the dust has settled, solutions are in place, and the issues have been rectified, if any negative attitude persists against you, link back to that trigger of the mistake and address this. It's best to set up a catch-up meeting and prepare the points that you want to raise.

During the meeting, you can indicate that you have sensed tension and want to work out the situation. If an apology is needed on your part, apologise, be polite and request their agreement to move on. If they are resistant to change or continue to maintain the ill-feeling, focus on getting on with your work journey. If they present challenges to you or your work, monitor the situation. If it becomes unprofessional or unworkable, you may need to raise it to a more senior manager or your Human Resources (HR) contact. Discuss it with your mentors and gather the best advice. Never accept bullying.

PART SIX

TIME FOR CHANGE?

The journey continues

CHAPTER 23

LEAVING WISELY

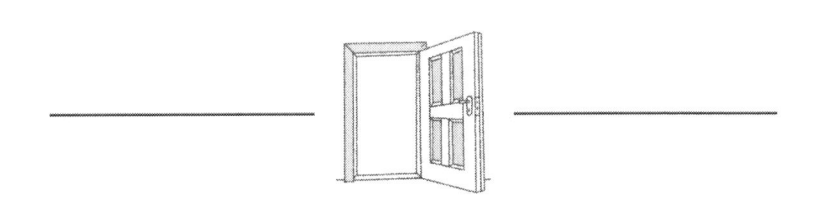

PEOPLE LEAVE JOBS FOR ALL KINDS OF REASONS. Some people make impulsive decisions after a tough period at work, others after a long thought-out process. Look out for the signals that it is time to move on. If a new opportunity is presented to you because someone has seen what you can do and is interested in you working for them, this is a clear sign that there are new horizons to be explored. Assess them well to make sure they are aligned to your goals and personal growth strategy.

Other reasons to leave include no longer feeling motivated or enthused by where you are, no longer learning anything new, or the job has become too easy. In such cases, you know you could be doing more. You have a desire within you to do something else or, possibly, there is tension within your team, and you are not developing.

Progression and movement, like rivers, are part of the natural rhythm of life. It's normal to move on to new roles - things that remain still can get stagnant. Get used to change, it is a part of life, nothing really stays completely constant – that would be boring and limited. Change is a good thing. A role that allows you to be lazy and go unchecked will affect you negatively in the long run. Wake up if you have been coasting. You are not improving in such a situation, you are stagnating!

Spend time to research and identify areas and roles that look like opportunities; this isn't always via the internal, or external job websites. It can also be from listening to strategy updates and listening out for areas of interest where expansion is taking place. You will be able to get that signal by following news about needing to grow teams, expand in regions, launch new projects or anywhere you hear a company has secured funding for growth. Intentionally following this kind of information directs you to where opportunities are. Though all teams and areas have new jobs and roles being created, when you get close to what the company's strategic priorities are, this is usually where you will find any new opportunities.

When an interesting job opportunity becomes available, there are careful approaches to take that differ, depending on whether it is internal or external. If it is external to your organisation, and you are keen to pursue it, keep all your plans and the interview process private, until you have completed the hiring process and have a concrete job offer in writing with the terms agreed from the new organisation. Schedule your interviews after work or at lunchtimes as far as possible and if you are successful in the interview and you want to go for the job offer that you received and accepted, wait for written confirmation before informing your manager.

You will usually then have to write a formal letter of resignation and will have a notice period to work off. One additional thing to note: if you're working in a sales or customer-facing role, some industries, particularly banking, if your new job offer is with a direct competitor organisation, your current employer may put you on leave from the day that you tell them you have a new job offer. This is because as the new employer is a competitor, you could now pose a threat because you have access to your current organisation's customer information.

If this kind of process occurs in the company you work with, your employer would place you on an immediate leave called *garden leave*. Work equipment would be collected and access to the organisation removed. The notice period is then worked without you doing any more work, hence the name *garden leave*. This can seem quite abrupt or harsh, but the organisation will be taking those actions to protect their information, whilst keeping you on and paying you for the period of your notice. When the notice period is complete, you would then officially leave and can begin your new job with the new organisation. Let's now move on to discussing internal opportunities and job moves.

In internal move situations, some companies require you to let your manager know that you're interviewing for roles as they may be contacted for a reference. You may be able to progress through the initial process to meet with contacts and see if it is warm first. I would suggest doing that so you can be more concrete that you are a strong candidate and at the same time make sure your manager is not caught by surprise. At the point you are ready to make a formal application for the role, book a meeting with your manager or arrange a catch-up.

After all the initial niceties, just like I covered in the preparation for promotion chapter, tell them that you are ready for a change and want to develop your experience. Then say you have found an internal role and you wanted to let them know that you are applying and would like their support. At this point, it may trigger their commitments to try and make you stay. Weigh up your options. Staying where you are or the new role: what is best for your progress and development? Remove all forms of sentiment or desire to please others.

If you decide you do want to pursue other internal opportunities, confirm that you will be going ahead and would like their support in the hiring process. That support can range from *basic support*, an awareness that you're interviewing and that's it, to *medium-level support*, knowing you're interviewing and preparing to give you a good reference, to *high-level support*, those who will be sad to see you go but understand that their role as a manager is to support you to progress.

The above approach can be very tricky. If you have a manager who you are not getting along with or a manager who really likes you - so much so that they would not want you to leave - both scenarios present a challenge and they may be reluctant to support you, offering the most basic level of engagement. That is why the timing of this conversation should be as far down the process as possible for you to be sure that that other role is looking like a possibility before you decide to mention it to your current boss. Once you mention that you are thinking of leaving, at all those levels of support, you become what is called a flight risk, an employee that could shortly be flying away (leaving).

The main thing to consider is that if there is likely to be some resentment about you moving on, as soon as your employer knows that you want to go, they may just leave you to it and start thinking about your replacement for their own protection. They will anticipate you could be gone in as little as a month or two and start already treating you like you have left before you have even secured the new job! You need to be wise. Unless you have a supportive manager who is helping you to progress, there is no point bringing up a new role that you are not sure about, or that you are not confident will actually result in a positive outcome.

I had to learn this early on in my career, when to my shock, I experienced a very senior manager destroy a job opportunity I had secured, just before it was finalised. In hindsight, in that situation, I should have fought for the role but instead, I just backed down and let it happen to me. That has not happened to me again since and I share it with you so that you are awake and can protect yourself. Current employers can potentially block or hamper internal moves. To avoid this, maintain a good relationship with your manager. Keep the other side warm and be prepared to professionally fight to secure what is yours if any funny business begins to transpire.

Be aware that colleagues at the same level can also get jealous and try and sabotage you. So be discreet. Don't share any of your plans to move, outside of those who actually need to know. In the team you're planning to leave, don't start talking about leaving or about how much you hate/dislike things. If the trigger for a move is irritation from a manager or unfair treatment, during the hiring process do not use the time as an opportunity to retaliate by giving poor performance or attitude during the application process. Bad attitudes when a person is departing can create negative effects later. The world of work gets smaller as you progress, and protecting your brand is very important.

How do you move wisely? By consistently doing a good job where you currently are until it's time to go! Leave in peace with your old team. As you are working your notice period, aim to make sure everything is complete as far as possible. Make sure you prepare high quality handover material and complete outstanding work as far as possible. Set up handover meetings and download all you need to explain to each of the team members taking over your responsibilities, or to new people who may have already been hired for your role. Always aim to leave a role positively to avoid negative things being said/remembered about you. This approach enhances your reputation, protects your brand and builds a strong legacy.

Your trusted mentors are your main go-to for internal job moves. Ideally the ones that are not in your business area. If you decide to confide in someone within your business area, be careful. Make sure it is just one other person who is not in competition with you but has more experience in the recruitment dynamics and who can support you. Such people fall into a middle group of people who can help you out. They can help you get you ready for success and even give you key information for you to research and prepare that will put you in a strong position in front of the hiring manager.

> **Wisdom nugget:**
>
> *It's always best to move from employed to new employment, rather than resigning into nothingness. Don't jump from a frying pan situation into a full-blown fire. Unless it is unbearable where you are, do not quit. Persevere so that you still receive your salary, but be focused, intentional and proactive about finding a new opportunity and making the right move.*

Now as your career progresses, the role usually becomes more senior; you are still the same person but what is required of you will be different. You are likely going to need to shift from seeing yourself as the youngest or most junior person, as that is likely to not be your role anymore. The next chapter looks at how you can accomplish this shift, and how you operate at a more senior level.

CHAPTER 24

LEADERSHIP - FROM JUNIOR TO SENIOR

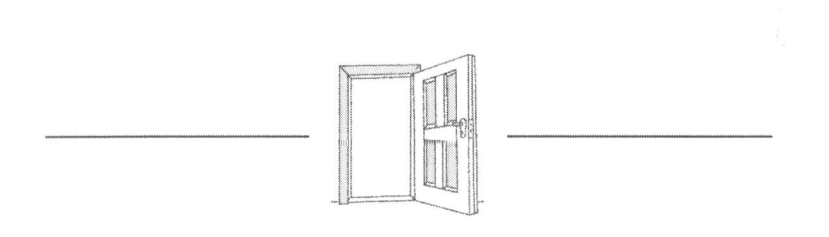

THIS SECTION WILL FURTHER SUPPORT YOU when you are transitioning from a junior to a more senior position. Becoming a boss! First thing - detach yourself from the mindset of being junior.

For those that start corporate careers early, real focus and taking the right steps can move you from being a *junior*, to rapidly developing the skill, experience, and energy to start overtaking the pace of those around you even though they are older or more senior to you. Seniority and position are not based on age. They are driven by demonstrating the attitude and experience required for a particular role. When you consistently produce quality output, maintain strong professional relationships and show a mature approach to work, you position yourself for more senior positions.

Be in preparation mode for moving upwards. Begin to practise shifting out of a junior mind-set. Be more confident with your thoughts and suggestions. This doesn't happen overnight but as you build more skill, experience and confidence in your abilities, you should start sharing your ideas more boldly. If you can see a way of improving a process or increasing the quality or value of something, clearly summarise your solution and share with your manager. Remember, when you share a new idea, it is highly likely you will have to play a role in implementing it. As far as possible support that effort, so it's not seen as you just creating work for others. If it improves output or creates a more efficient approach, you will also get the credit and demonstrate more of your value. These are the things that you can then use as your evidence when discussing your impact and putting yourself forward for new opportunities.

Being more assertive is important when moving from a *junior to a senior role*. It's not just about speaking up more. It's about speaking up with wisdom and confidence. When you share a suggestion, it's not just calling out the problem but also showing that you have thought about the solution and are now communicating that you have a plan for how to achieve it. It's about showing that you have looked at a problem from all angles and have decided on a suitable suggestion.

For more complex ideas, before sharing them with your manager, you may want to first get some feedback from more senior team members to check if the idea sounds viable. During this validation process, just be mindful, as some colleagues may not be as enthusiastic about your idea or may not be as open to new ways of working. In the opposite scenario, others may like your idea so much that they actually take it and personally run with it themselves! Unless you are working on a team project, where idea sharing is critical for team success, be selective about how widely you share the ideas you want to personally create or contribute, to demonstrate what you can do. Mentors are a great sounding board for getting advice on the best way to land your ideas for the greatest impact with your managers or others.

When it comes to putting your point across via email, moving from a more junior tentative position to a more senior assertive position would be "Could we possibly" to "I would suggest that we..." Or "I think we could" to "We should look at..." In each case, the shift is one from being unsure and cautious to being sure of yourself and ready to contribute. What should be avoided, is rushing to speak on a matter without proper consideration, or confidently trying to contribute to a situation you do not fully understand. Both scenarios could really embarrass you if you end up being wrong. The senior approach is to be more considered, informed, assertive and professional.

When you move up to a more senior role within the same business area, there can be colleagues who previously worked with you, who still see you as junior. This could show up in various ways. You might not be included on emails that you should be seeing in your new position. Or you may not be informed about things you should know about in your new role. In some cases, it may just be colleagues forgetting to include you. That happens, especially early on in new roles. On rare occasions it may be intentional but you will find that very difficult to confirm. Regardless of the reasoning, it is important to raise/call out any instances professionally. "Please, could you forward me the email and keep me on copy for all future emails on the subject?"; "Please, could you add me to the meeting invite?"; "Please, let me know the outcome of xxx." There is no need to be demanding or rude. Just be clear, confident and ask for access to the information you need for your new role and inclusion into the spaces that you are entitled to be in.

When you secure a more senior role, there can be feelings of not being qualified enough, viewing the new role as a mountain and potentially feeling unsupported by your colleagues who expect you to be able to get on without assistance. This can create a feeling of vulnerability when you need help, fearing to ask questions and the creation of many negative thoughts whizzing around. It all just knocks your confidence. This feeling has actually been termed "*imposter syndrome*" - feeling like a fraud, like you don't really have what it takes and questioning your abilities and past successes. It is a feeling that you will be exposed as being inadequate and incapable. These are limiting beliefs and need to be caught and reversed. You can do it. Shake off the lies and tell yourself, "I can do this!"

Just keep in mind the fact that all roles involve new learning, regardless of your previous experience. A new role is a new level, so it is always a new start. You will have to expand your capacity and you grow fastest by reading around your subject and studying how those around you work. Engage with your senior mentors to help you break down your approach to more challenging situations and your new responsibilities. Closely watch how the environment around you operates. Focus on presenting your points with confidence and being open to input and feedback. That way, you are continually being shaped as your role progresses.

After you have pushed those lying feelings of inadequacy to the side, be ready to push any external negativity to the side too. Some may see you and make a judgment on you, or challenge you based on nothing but bias or unfamiliarity to you in that capacity. It can be on anything from age, race, ethnicity, gender, perceived inexperience, etc. and you may not be able to confidently pinpoint what the exact issue is. Just focus on limiting your interaction with people operating like that and, when you do interact, focus on the quality of your work being the silencer in such cases. Also, keep your mentors close to help you to navigate such situations. Don't let yourself engage in any negative or frustration-led conversations. You have been chosen to step up. Keep going.

There will be greater expectations from you as you become more senior. Without warning, a manager could contact you for information that they expect you to know straight away. They may need the information urgently or could be testing you to see how prepared you are. Keep their cares in your mind. Start training your brain to remember information that you are responsible for – numbers/dates/results. Build the habit and discipline of staying close to the key numbers and in addition to that - stay on top of your email inbox! Make sure you listen attentively when your manager is speaking. That blank stare after you have been bamboozled by questions, can be hilarious but you don't want to be the clown. Pay attention when your boss is talking, focus. If you don't know the answer, simply say, "I'll check and get back to you in [a realistically rapid period]" and that is perfectly fine.

In a more senior position, you are expected to be less dependent on your manager telling you what to do. You are expected to set more of the direction for what needs to be done. If you are elevated within a team, it requires a switch in your mind and operate as a manager. You are expected to exercise more authority and have greater clarity on what needs to happen. Again, *not over confidence or arrogance.* Bring the team around you into your ideas in a collaborative way, not a commanding way. Check in with your manager and be open to different views and wider consultation across your team, as well as demonstrating leadership.

Moving from a junior to a more senior role requires a mental shift for sure. Own your new level of responsibility. Intentionally put in place the other elements we have journeyed through in this book; the attitude for acceleration, managing your brand, building on your strengths and managing your weaknesses, keeping your focus, being visible, managing your work relationships, maintaining a strong network of mentors and sponsors and always being open to growth opportunities.

It is a learning process, so don't put too much pressure on yourself to be perfect. It takes time and sometimes you may feel out of your depth. That is normal. Leverage the approaches shared throughout the book to give you that best practice boost but also remember to connect with your colleagues and professional support system, and take time out to rest when needed and release any pressure. Development is all about having a willingness to be stretched into a higher level of your greatness. Keep growing and celebrate your successes along the way too.

In the next chapter, we will be looking at the opportunity to lead as just that – an opportunity. Moving into a position of leadership can really feel like an achievement but it also requires different strategies and approaches to optimally handle the new level of responsibility. Let's explore this in more detail.

CHAPTER 25

BECOMING A MANAGER

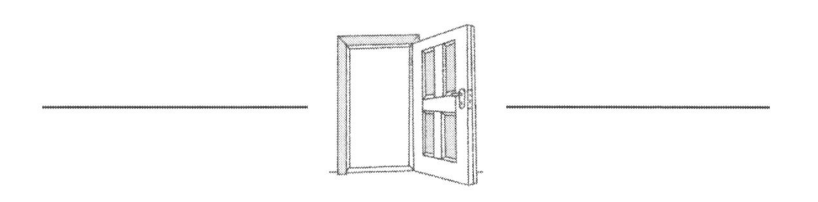

THE ROLE OF A TEAM LEADER is sandwiched between two very thick slices of corporate bread. Above you, there are the senior managers to whom you are accountable for a piece of work or a project, but as a team leader you will not always be doing the work you are responsible for delivering. Instead you have more responsibility for managing the team and delivering the necessary quality. It is a big responsibility that some get wrong and some get right.

The right approach to team management: dos and don'ts:

- Never let the opportunity to lead or manage others inflate you with pride and arrogance. Those people you have the opportunity to manage, may one day become your managers.

- Your role as a team leader is to be responsible for the output and be able to delegate tasks and manage the productivity of your team. As a manager, you need to plan ahead and prepare the steps the team need to follow.

- You must be clear on the tasks you need to set, for you to achieve future desired output from your team. You also need to be very close to the detail of what is happening across your team and each person's work and deliverables so you can keep your managers informed.

- When you're leading a team, you have to know when to be a pal and when to be a boss. If you are too friendly, you will find it hard to be firm when you need to be.

- An active manager is one that is intentional about the work and the team.

- You are in a position of responsibility for the team members' personal development.

- You will therefore also need to train your team members and help each individual develop.

- Deal with any challenging issues that the team under you can't face and collate summaries to update those in charge of you about the overall message about where you are as a team.

- In such a role, you will regularly be required to check the progress of the team, challenge poor performance and turn around any areas of work or individuals who are slacking.

- You should also be prepared to lead by example and demonstrate your own work ethic and the behaviour that you are encouraging your team to demonstrate.

Nobody likes to be bossed around, disrespected, or made to feel small. As a leader, determine that you will not treat people like that. Whatever level a person is at, they are working to support your work. They are there to contribute to the overall business and deserve to be treated with respect. You also have an output to deliver and they are a part of that and need to be guided by clear requests. Sometimes you need to assert leadership in your position. If you treat people with respect and demonstrate vision and inspiration, people will follow. When issues arise, you need to accelerate productivity, be professional and factual about what needs to be done and the impact of low quality, or deadlines being missed. Be constructive and supportive; agree on targets to monitor progress.

If you are authoritarian, it can cause resistance or fear. You may therefore have people working for you but not wanting to work *with* you. In such cases, you have control but it's likely that the output will not be the best you could receive. When you show that you have a focus on the team and you make sure that everybody is seen, given recognition, and celebrated when they achieve or contribute, you are likely to get better results from them as they will also feel valued. Direct your team. Don't leave them in the middle of nowhere. Be willing to teach and empower. Clarify anything that doesn't make sense so that with their confidence built, they can stand on their own two feet. Give feedback to help shape their development and be willing to receive feedback on how you can also improve. Being open to receiving feedback also helps you build a connection with the team.

Another thing to bear in mind is the method of correction or driving improvement in a team member. If someone you are managing makes a mistake, do not address their error publicly, especially not in front of your seniors. It will humiliate them, damage their reputation, and likely cause them to build resentment towards you. It also does not reflect well on you as a manager. Rather than shielding your employee, it will come across as you protecting yourself, whereas a manager is supposed to protect and cover their team.

By not shielding your employee it demonstrates a more junior way of behaving: individualism and calling out the errors of others publicly to make yourself look more competent and capable. It also demonstrates a lack of management development. It is therefore always better to have a one-to-one conversation with your employee, to understand and address the issue at hand and ensure your points are understood. You should see it as an opportunity both to correct and coach them to improve.

If any performance issue is more serious or prolonged, and your one-to-ones do not change anything; discuss with your senior manager in private. Take on their recommendations for how to encourage positive change, have clear targets as you need to drive a quick change and result from the employee as a return for the investment being made in them. If there is still no change it may be a case to involve HR. I would also suggest that before taking that action you also discuss the seriousness with the employee and provide a pre-warning so that they have a final opportunity to make a change. If they don't do so and disciplinary consequences follow, the individual will have to accept their responsibility. There will be minimal room to complain about unfairness or even discrimination as you will have demonstrated management values, transparency, and fairness.

Finally, as a team leader or manager, beware of how you treat rising talent within your team. When your team member is shining, don't discourage or keep them down. Encourage what you see by giving them more responsibility, but also making sure they stay within the structure of the team. Beware of feeling intimidated or insecure because of rising talent in your team. Everyone has an individual race in life and each one runs at a different pace.

If you recognise someone is much more capable than the role they are in, rather than feeling threatened, which can happen especially if there is arrogance, irrespective of their attitude, your role is to develop their talent. Train them to increase their capabilities and give them parts of your role to support. Coach them on their behaviours and try and help them find an opportunity to shine, develop and build their own team. That good act may also come around to benefit you in the future.

Now management has been a prominent factor throughout the book so far. It has not really needed its own chapter, as the general expectation is that managers are there to give you the opportunity to develop, support your progress and obtain the benefits of you contributing strongly to their team. Managers in most cases are supportive. Even at points when you need to challenge them for your reward and recognition, it is understood to be part of business and should be dealt with in a professional way, regardless of the ultimate decision. There are, however, instances where the relationship can break down and this can be for a range of reasons from trivial to more serious – a personality clash, a mistake made, low performance, or a bias they have resulting in unfair treatment or discrimination.

In the next chapter, I will share strategies to manage yourself through tougher periods, where there is conflict with your manager. I sincerely hope that the advice shared will help you keep in mind the choices you have and enable you to make wise moves that enable you to reach optimum outcomes.

CHAPTER 26

MANAGERS – SUPPORTIVE vs. UNSUPPORTIVE

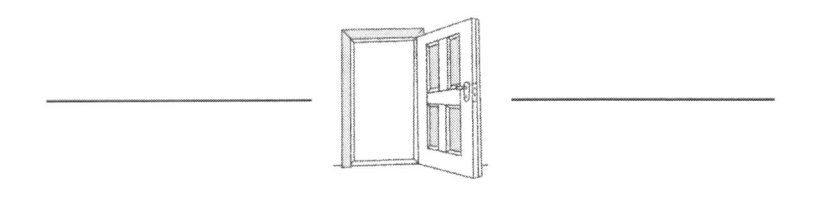

IN A JOB, THERE IS A TWO-WAY PAYOFF. You are solving a problem for the company, your team and your manager by delivering value and doing your job well. In return, you should have a supportive manager, access to training and development opportunities as well as your salary. Optimal situations occur when you have a supportive manager who is committed to managing you intentionally. This kind of manager is interested in your career development, not just in how well you are doing in your job. There are some who will be willing to teach you everything they know and push you to the highest of heights, being there as your back up and building your confidence along the way. If you come across such a manager, it is a gift. Value that gift, and learn as much as you can from them and the way that they work.

As you spend such a large part of life working, it should be an enjoyable process or at least professional, polite and one that brings value to your life. During busy, more pressurised moments at work, managers may be more abrupt, or firmer in their tone. We are all human and so this can happen during more intense seasons, but it should not occur on a regular basis, and you should not accept being insulted or treated unprofessionally.

If it ever starts to feel like you are consistently receiving negativity, being completely unsupported, even possibly being bullied or treated unprofessionally, this is a cause for concern. It is not something you should allow yourself to get comfortable with. Staying in such an environment will sap your energy, affect your ability to deliver and could even affect your mental health and emotional wellness.

As soon as things feel like they are negatively shifting, the first thing to do is check yourself; it is always best to start there so you can remove all responsibility for the issues from yourself. Then you can clearly see what other forces may be driving the negativity. As you are in their team, you have made a commitment to supporting the progress of the team and the business area. The organisation ultimately requires you to do a good job, so don't let your work slip or miss deadlines for work or activities that you are expected to complete. In some cases, there may be a personality clash with a manager. Though this is likely to cause frustration, remember that all your engagements at work should be professional and civil, even in a disagreement.

If you do fall out with your boss, in a situation that has the potential to get heated, there are a few solutions:

1. Check yourself and take a moment to calm down. Never be pushed to lose your temper.

2. When you are calm, be committed to reconciling. You could organise a meeting/coffee to discuss the situation. See if the response is one that is supportive and committed to rebuilding constructively.

3. If you observe a willingness to rebuild, give them that opportunity and don't harbour a grudge. Address the issues and reach an amicable resolution. Then decide to put it behind you.

4. If the situation deteriorates and you start to experience negativity towards yourself, note the instances. If you see no improvement, you should bring these situations to their attention as a first response.

5. If you have brought a series of examples to their attention but the situation isn't acknowledged and deteriorates further, you may need to escalate to a more senior manager or if very serious, to HR.

Please be intentional about keeping your professionalism in the optimal place – stay cool. Issues and tense conversations occur at work, especially with conflicting priorities and limited time. Please aim not to take things personally and to move past tense conversations with a solid focus on getting the job done.

I learned that being able to move past disagreements professionally, without holding a grudge or ill feeling, was part of maturing in a role and in your career.

Now for whatever reason, if there ever becomes a point where you or your manager remains hostile, that is never acceptable. There are also cases where a manager may or may not be hostile or just not interested in your development or career progression. They may have a minimal desire to develop or nurture your talent. The first sign of a toxic situation is repeated conflicts with your manager. If you somehow end up with such a manager and you are in a role where you are still developing your capability and experience, you will need to make a change, or change your approach, to avoid being negatively impacted.

During your developing phase, an extended period with this type of manager could significantly damage your career progression/confidence. You risk being made to look stupid regularly because of your limited experience and no support being provided. They may not have any interest in training or upskilling you because they just enjoy the ego boost of having someone working for them. No real direction and being given tasks that seem to add no value, but you can't confidently push back on them. I experienced this just a few times but, on the occasions that it happened, it was tough. I also supported a few colleagues through challenging times with their managers. An unsupportive, hostile environment can seriously affect your growth and wellbeing.

If you find yourself in that type of situation, you really have three options initially:

1. Stay and just focus on getting your job done, keeping a boundary; during the bad experience, identify a great manager or mentor who can be trusted and with whom you have a solid relationship and share the situation for professional advice. Even if you want to vent, calm down first. Don't have an outburst. Always try and deliver the message in a way that is professional and cannot be used against you. It can be hard, especially where there is a lot of frustration, but be wise.

2. Be patient. Get what you can out of the role and be zealous about securing another job opportunity. You can even reach out to previous managers and go back to your previous team as a quick and, possibly, easier move if there is an opening. If that is not an option, continue to build relationships around you and in the area you are interested in. Think about where your skills could compliment and directly ask if there are opportunities and just go for it and apply. This is a sideways path that could be internal or external. It may take you in a different direction but with a good manager and or a better working environment you will feel better about work and may even have more access to training and new skills.

3. If the behaviour starts to shift into bullying, or you are clearly being treated in an unprofessional way, rather than being forced to find another job or leave, you could also raise the issue with HR. Before doing so, speak with

a mentor outside of your immediate business area for advice. You may then want to raise this first informally with HR for guidance on your options. An HR escalation, like raising a grievance against your manager, would be your entitlement, but as this action is a formal, official process, this could introduce more friction, and it's often more of a last resort. Get guidance first.

Nobody at work has the right to operate as a bully, be rude or unprofessional. Don't accept this behaviour. You don't have to tolerate it. It is not a requirement for progress. To more immediately address a heated conversation or surprise negative remark, keep your cool and simply say, "You cannot speak to me in that manner. I will not be continuing this conversation if you cannot address me professionally." Don't kick off in an explosion. You will look terrible and even though they are the cause, you will be the one that looks like you are in the wrong. If you come across this character type, don't fear them. Set your boundaries and keep a note of unacceptable actions.

A consistently negative relationship with your manager can start affecting your attitude, motivation and even the quality of your work. What you don't want, is a negative work situation to result in a poor performance review against you which would affect your ability to progress. If the working situation really deteriorates, remember you have options. In some cases, where you do not want to leave a role or do not have another role to move to, the decision can be made to formally escalate to HR. This is usually viewed as the worst-case scenario, last resort and final stage in workplace battling.

A common example is to raise a grievance against the manager. This makes things serious but where it is warranted, it is a process that exists to protect employees and address unacceptable behaviour. HR involvement is an area that most of us try to avoid as it can be an uncomfortable process and inevitably creates some form of tension. Without a doubt, all employees are entitled to engage with HR when facing difficult workplace situations and should never just suffer in silence. We will look at this in more detail, within the next chapter.

CHAPTER 27

HR - CASES AND STRATEGIES

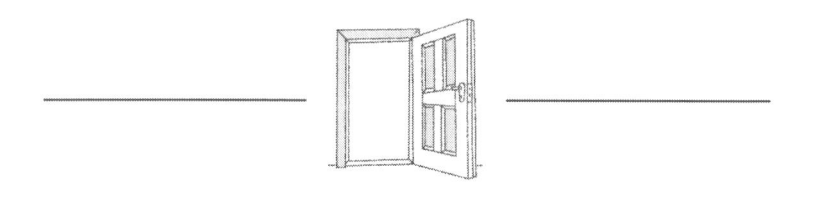

THE HUMAN RESOURCES (HR) DEPARTMENT governs all the people-related aspects within a company but aside from the hiring process, you don't usually have too many direct engagements with them. Your manager usually receives guidance and cascades anything you require. Direct dealings with HR might occur when you want to discuss any personal benefits that you may be entitled to, you want to find out about working within another location or sort out your personal profile within HR systems. Usually, HR also creates avenues to enable you to discuss confidential matters related to your role or team.

On the other hand – if things have turned negative in a role, HR can also become directly involved in the matter. If you need to raise a serious complaint (grievance) against a team member or manager for treatment at work over a period of time that is unfair, unprofessional and ultimately negative towards you, this is usually called *raising a grievance*. Likewise, if you haven't been performing optimally yourself for a while, failed to meet improvement targets your manager has set or been involved in some form of poor conduct, a disciplinary procedure involving HR can be initiated by your manager.

HR disciplinary procedures can also arise against you if a serious error is made at work. A compliance failure, security breaches, or anything deemed as serious misconduct could be a trigger. Now we should all be working with integrity and following the rules on conduct, behaviour, and compliance - that is just a given. If rules are broken there are consequences, which could involve HR disciplinary procedures or even being fired if the situation is extremely serious. That is a reality, and one to keep in mind. The severity of punishment in some cases is there to deter employees from putting the organisation, customers, or themselves at risk.

Formal HR procedures will usually be recorded on your performance management documentation, like a bad stain. It negatively affects the internal view of a candidate, hindering progression, until it is removed. This is all the more reason to manage yourself well, do what you need to be doing on time and maintain the professionalism outlined throughout this book in order to never find yourself in such a situation.

In some instances, where there is negligence and mistakes are made, these more serious HR cases can arise so be very careful and avoid anything that is risky or that you are unsure about.

There are some situations where there is a breakdown in the manager and employee relationship, made worse by the employee not delivering the highest standard of work. This is the worst situation to fall into because your manager will just have too much power. The gap in performance creates an opening for the manager to build an HR case against you.

In cases like this, there may be other underlying negative biases operating but that is masked by the evidence of poor work from the employee, so that can seem to justify the process. Where there is a negative relationship with a manager and/or there is no fall in work output or the employee is performing in line with the rest of the team and formal HR procedures are raised, this more strongly points to targeted negativity, especially if there seems to have been a significantly harsher approach or more severe action taken against one colleague in comparison to others.

This disproportionate treatment could point to discrimination, which unfortunately still occurs in workplaces, but it is very difficult to concretely prove when it is not overt and explicit. If any of these situations occur for whatever reason and result in you having to enter a formal HR meeting, the following are the *woke tools* I would suggest for you to prepare yourself to progress through the process as safely as possible.

See ten key steps below:

1. Ask to bring in an independent witness. This added element encourages more balance and professionalism in the meeting. As disciplinary meetings can be very stressful, you can ask for an advocate, spokesperson or trade union

representative to be allowed to attend and listen in, or even speak on your behalf if the process feels too stressful.

2. Request an independent note-taker to document the whole meeting and send you all the notes. The presence of these added participants creates more witnesses, so it naturally encourages the process to be delivered more fairly and objectively. You don't need all three. Usually there is at most one representative and one note-taker.

3. Keep your facts organised and well documented.

4. Gather information from witnesses and other stakeholders who can support your case.

5. Stay calm, stay focused and breathe deeply. The actual meetings can be very daunting because of their negative and confrontational nature.

6. At the point you enter the room, whether it is a disciplinary situation or a grievance, don't look like the victim or like you are guilty as charged.

7. Rehearse what you are going to say with your mentors and trusted colleagues, family members or friends who are working in the HR space and who can guide you.

8. If you are the one raising the case as a grievance against a manager because of unfair treatment, discrimination, or any other misconduct, state the facts without adding emotion.

9. Present calmly, structure your argument and don't ramble. Make your points succinctly, then stop and be silent. Remember to breathe, to release tension and stay focused.

10. Seek advice and do your research - HR should be there to advise you as well as your manager on the company policy and process. Request your HR policies and procedures to read and ask your HR representative questions in advance so you know what to expect. In addition, seek external advice for additional support. This can include finding a union representative who can support you. Good sources for further information include:

The citizens advice bureau -
https://www.citizensadvice.org.uk/work/
The employment advice bureau –
https://www.employment-advice-bureau.org/

If allegations against you are serious, you may want to seek independent legal advice prior to the meeting.

When you have a disciplinary for poor performance – remain calm and prepare to work!

If you have been brought into a disciplinary conversation because your manager isn't happy with you or your performance, depending on how justified you view that to be, if you feel it is unfair it can leave you boiling on the inside. I have certainly experienced this, where an initial personality clash with a manager who took on the leadership of our team after a previous manager departed, turned into a very toxic situation. Public ridicule in meetings, minimal support and nothing short of bullying became the usual experience with this manager. As our working relationship worsened, this culminated in a formal disciplinary procedure being initiated against me to monitor my work and overall performance. Ouch!

This being very early on in my career, it completely hit me by surprise. I already expected the bad ratings as this manager was never satisfied with what I did. Nothing was ever good enough, but I had never come across a performance improvement process and never been in any form of disciplinary procedure. It was HR explaining to me what my manager had initiated that brought it all life. Ultimately, I was given a three-month probation period, with specific targets to hit and, if I passed, I could keep my job and if I failed, something more severe, possibly even job loss.

That meeting was like a nightmare - like being in a courtroom on trial for a crime I knew I wasn't guilty of, but the prosecution just had it in for me. Just sitting nervously in the dock knowing that a whole system I did not even understand had just been unleashed against me. Full set of charges firmly lodged and me just sitting there, representing myself, cornered and unable to adequately present a counter argument. My weak defence versus my manager and the HR jury vying for my downfall. It was a disaster! I was just not prepared at all.

I had no idea at that time, that a breakdown in relationship with your manager could result in them utilising the system to get rid of you procedurally. Continuing the analogy, after I had received my three-month sentence, I had a moment of deep reflection. I had three options - give up, get angry or get out of the mess. I chose the latter and worked like a machine. I was adamant to overturn both the charges and the performance improvement plan sentence. I felt it was completely unfair and I needed justice and my freedom.

During that first month of the performance improvement plan period, I literally attacked every single target. I tapped into my turbo-drive and worked at a speed and passion I had not experienced since the role had turned so negative and toxic. I was working to reinstate my personal honour, dignity and reputation. It was not about the manager or the performance improvement plan, it was about me and what I knew I was capable of. I did not allow for any mistakes in my work. I anticipated every situation, worked beyond every expectation, finished my work early and to a high standard, and then took on additional areas of work that would increase my visibility.

Within three weeks, that three-month performance improvement plan had already been made redundant by my performance. Within four weeks it was completely cancelled! It was totally unjustified given the work I had achieved. One of the business areas that I had been supporting during the performance improvement plan period, had a role come up a few months later. They had valued my work for them, my focus and they wanted me in their team. Within two months of what felt like an attempted sabotage of my career by that manager, I had been offered a new job that came with a promotion and pay rise. How is that for vindication?

I really hope that story serves to encourage anyone who is going through tough career moments, disciplinary or performance improvement processes. Whether you are guilty or not, you do not have to stay in the negativity of the situation. You can refocus, recharge, and start shifting a negative situation to a positive one. In my story, you will also see that I did not engage in any confrontational battling. That would have been petty and unprofessional. It is just not worth it. I protected my personal brand and let my work and networking do the battling, staying full of faith and focused to overcome the challenge.

Though I hope you will not have to go through a disciplinary procedure, if you do find yourself being summoned for an initial disciplinary meeting, just keep in mind that it will require inner strength. It is a meeting that will require you to defend yourself, so in preparation, gather and organise as many facts about performance/results as required to confidently support how you are delivering against your targets and gather feedback as evidence for where you are viewed positively by other managers or colleagues.

During the meeting, the toughest part is having to hear the various negative points raised against you. Nobody likes to listen to criticism so the temptation may arise to argue back and call the claims untrue, etc. Rather than doing that and self-control needs to be activated to avoid you being triggered to behave in a way that makes you come across negatively and back up negative points against you. Instead, just take deep breaths if needed to stay calm, listen to the points and take notes. At the end when they have finished, just say, "I disagree with xxx" and present the facts you have as calmly as possible. It can be very frustrating but try to keep your composure.

Before you go into that situation, it's worthwhile spending some time to practise what you're going to say. The more you practise, the more what you need to say will come out naturally and with confidence when you actually say it. Before you go into those meetings also be clear about the positive outcome that you want to have at the end of the meeting. Imagine that positive outcome and the situation going in your favour. I have also found it helpful to pray about it, too.

If the outcome is positive – wonderful, don't rub it in with your manager, just maintain your dignity and focus on maintaining a professional working relationship for as long as you remain in that role. If the outcome is negative, it does not have to be a permanent predicament as you saw in my case. Only you know what you are truly capable of, so for as long as you are there, work to have the warning lifted, the performance improvement plan satisfied and closed whilst demonstrating your value. Don't settle for the outcome defining you. It may seem like a mountain but just focus, do what you need to do to conquer it, and learn from the experience, so you don't have to repeat the process again. As I saw, positive things can even come out of it.

Now *you* remain the most important factor in your career and in this whole process. If HR is involved formally between you and your manager or you and another colleague, this usually has a very damaging impact on ongoing working relationships. The situation may improve, but often when HR procedures are involved, it is a signal that it may be wise to make a move and go where there is a demand for you, rather than staying in a negative environment, just being tolerated. Go where you can flourish, as well as develop in your career. The optimal situation is finding a role that pays you more and offers you new experiences. If you decide that you need to move on, what may happen initially is that you find a role you want but it pays slightly less. Decide if you are willing to take a pay cut for more peace and an open path to progress. It isn't healthy to operate in a tense culture of fear or frustration. Concentrate on doing what is best for you, your wellbeing, and your career journey.

PART SEVEN

THE NEW NORMAL, PRIVACY AND NETWORKS

Adapt accordingly

CHAPTER 28

BEING *WOKE AT WORK* IN A VIRTUAL WORLD

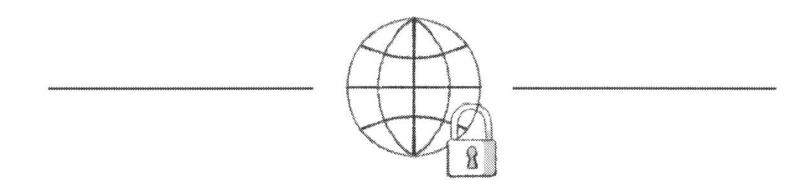

THE YEAR 2020 FIRMLY USHERED in the digital transformation of workplace interaction. The onset of COVID-19 was tragic for many families who lost loved ones, and the normality of work in offices was disrupted and transformed into widespread virtual working. This required people to get tech-savvy quickly and start to conduct their work engagement in a virtual way. This seemed optimal, working from home, not having to deal with the workplace dynamics of managers and colleagues, and all the relationships we have just mentioned, but it brought our personal worlds right into the office. We became accustomed to hearing children and pets on calls, deliveries as online shopping replaced visiting retail outlets. As a result, a much-heightened level of accommodating each other emerged which was welcomed. This reduced a layer of seriousness and increased the sense of us all being in it together.

A few months into the lockdown, digital working was being termed as the *new normal*. Professionalism and how to connect with your organisation was rapidly being redefined. As the evolution and adaptations continued, there were many concerns about how to progress and engage with managers and teams in a virtual world. It was all still possible, during the various lockdowns, as people were sadly made redundant, other people were being hired, promoted, given pay rises and generally progressing. Though the forms of contact with employers are becoming more virtual in nature, the professional principles still matter, arguably even more so. I will share suggestions on what you can do to make sure you are showing up in your best light and positioning yourself for progress within the virtual workplace.

VIRTUAL PROFESSIONALISM

Still keep up that protection of your brand. Integrity still stands. If you are supposed to be present at a meeting, delivering work or making a call, don't slack. Join your virtual meetings on time or early, don't be in the habit of joining late or missing them. I have observed many people just not showing up. Possibly getting fed up with constant calls and not seeing the value in them. Just note - it may not be called out directly but that does not mean it is going unnoticed. In the background, managers are on calls with each other daily, navigating how to weather the crisis periods and manage costs. These seemingly minor things can work against you. Don't be on their minds for the wrong reasons.

Now whatever connectivity platform your company is using, you will have the option to switch on your camera for calls. My recommendation is - ALWAYS start calls with your camera set to "off" so you are not caught by surprise. If you are going to switch on your camera, have reasonably professional attire on (not your pyjamas) and position yourself in front of a plain wall, with a window to the side or in front of you for some natural light. Do not have a window directly behind you with your camera on. It will make you appear like a dark shadow on the camera or a silhouette.

Upload a professional/presentable picture of yourself onto your connectivity platform (Zoom, MS Teams, Google Meet, etc.); that then gives you a professional cover which enables others to see you even on days when you may not have even had the chance to get fully ready. You may also want to join using a background effect or virtual background. This will enable your background to be completely blurred out with a virtual setting and only you to be seen. Great if your living space is a bit messy.

MUTE! Join your meeting connectivity platform on mute. It just protects you from sounds, interruptions or distractions that can feed in from your world into your group calls. The worst is when you think you're on mute, a call comes in and you start talking and see on the screen "The host has muted you." Embarrassing! Just aim to get into that habit of muting when you are not presenting and of course, listening out in case you are required to contribute. One of the most common meeting phrases is, "Sorry I was on mute." Remember to unmute to speak!

If you are leading a virtual meeting, join ten minutes early to test the connection and make sure everything is working. By being early you also ensure that your attendees are not waiting for you at the start of the meeting. If you are in another meeting that is likely to overrun and cause you to be late to your own meeting, it is better to excuse yourself from that one so that you can be on time for your own. If it is one that you can't leave, then out of courtesy, send an email to your meeting attendees to explain you are running late and when you will start the call.

Managers are doing more team check-ins and update calls in the virtual working environment. The intention is to check in more personally to ensure employee wellbeing. Note - your boss asks you what your week is looking like, focus on the work you are required to be delivering and update on that. Treat that question it like it was asked in the office. I have observed colleagues becoming very casual on this and mentioning lazy days or empty schedules. Don't do this.

Be *woke* my friends. This shift will require you to be on top of your game. Don't get sucked in by all the sentiment flowing around. When an organisation needs to survive, they will make tough decisions and at a time like this your virtual and digital engagement is vital, as well as making sure you don't leave anything undone that can be used against you.

Mandatory online training or learning - this is one of the core assessments that is catching up with people. These can be left until the last minute or fall into overdue as you work on other day-to-day responsibilities. Make sure you are up to date on everything you need to complete to do your job.

The events of 2020 ushered in a more distanced management style: managers making tough decisions based on data and having a digital interface that avoids human connection and emotion.

KEEPING UP YOUR ENGAGEMENT VIRTUALLY

This again starts with punctual presence and being prepared for the virtual check-ins that will be organised by your business.

Make sure your mobile devices are charged, and during your workday, ensure your work phone is near you. As your presence is not seen, it is your online presence and ease of contacting you that now counts for seeing you in the office. Picking up your calls after one ring, etc. looks good. Missed calls look bad.

Don't see it as being tracked but as you showing up - that is the basic part. The real engagement part is you having something meaningful to say on calls. Unfortunately, even those who previously would have just been shy and quiet, now also need to speak up in team meeting and group call settings. Keep it brief, no waffle.

Now be proactive about calling your manager and putting in a one-to-one check in every two weeks, for example, or even weekly. Don't just disappear into the virtual universe. It is easy to do but again, be ahead of the game. Keep yourself on your manager's radar in a balanced and regular way, not in their face and not missing. Use the time to update them on your world and ask them about any updates they have on how things are progressing or how the strategic focus is evolving.

In terms of your engagement, you can think of things you can do to support your manager and team. This could be through showing awareness of various things the team needs to get done and ensure everyone is reminded about it. Share useful links such as upcoming deadlines on training that most will have forgotten, or information about initiatives/applications that some may have missed. Share tips on how you have completed something the team has to do, or links to new employee benefits you have come across. Just maintain a balance. Don't make that your full-time job; you are not the PA of the team. These are just some ideas of good things to do from time to time that position you as someone useful, organised and on top of things.

As many things are moving thick and fast, if you hear your manager say they need to get something done for the whole team, just get the piece done offline (away from the public forum so you don't come across as a people-pleaser), and email your manager to say, "Sorted this out and happy to share with the team." You will have saved them the extra hassle and it just goes towards your credibility. Also, being available to join team calls or cover colleagues are also ways of showing your contribution.

NETWORKING IN A VIRTUAL WORLD

This one is tricky but not impossible. What I have noticed now, is that everyone has been brought closer through the digital nature of business. Everything is a lot more accessible. It's the same location, all of us now meeting via our phones or computers.

As with any networking, you should have an intentional attitude towards it. For networking, join events that your team is holding such as larger team meetings, conference calls and town hall/department wide meeting. If there is an opportunity for Q&A, take your opportunity to ask that question. When you hear a response to your question, following that, you could reach out directly to request a 15 min catch-up on something further, or to develop the point you raised on the call and use that for further networking.

It also doesn't even need to be another call; you can just share via email with the person. State that after hearing them speaking at this or that event, you have put together something that you think could add value. Share your ideas and your solutions.

This is a more organic route than just firing off an email cold. If they are not at the highest levels of seniority then, just like with your manager, you can request a quick catch-up meeting. But it is important to be able to share what you would like to discuss and ensure it isn't too long; twenty minutes is ideal as it gives them time to prepare for their next meeting.

CAREER PROGRESSION IN A VIRTUAL WORLD

The thing I will say is that feedback is critical. First of all, make sure you are delivering value and doing a good job; then make sure you get external feedback on your performance to raise awareness about how others view your work. There are often time a colleague or client may say some wonderful things about you or your work after you have delivered something. Just ask if they would send that to you in an email and then you can forward that on to your manager. The targets you achieve and the feedback received is what is needed to speak on your behalf, rather than you alone sharing how well you are doing.

I often struggled with requesting and sharing great feedback with my managers. I felt that sharing praise about my work was boasting and should be kept private. It's actually the opposite. Feedback is another indicator to your manager about your performance. It celebrates what you have done and recognises your effort. This should not be seen as boasting and if you have felt like this, please remove that interpretation. When you receive great feedback, it's because you have done a great job! Gather your positive written feedback, create an email folder to store it when received and make sure you share it with your manager. Use your positive feedback to support your performance and salary review conversations.

You should also send positive feedback via email to other colleagues who have done something exceptional and even to your manager if they have done something that goes above and beyond to support you. For feedback emails, you can send them directly to the person or copy in their managers for greater visibility.

If you have other stakeholders who have supported you or who have an interest in you as talent, you can also share feedback with them. If it is confidential work or external client feedback you may need to just advise them more generally about the nature of the feedback to protect the client's privacy. Fundamentally, you will be using the feedback to support your career progression. Follow the exact steps in the mid-year review section. It's the same fundamentals as the prior sections on progress and promotion.

So now that we have taken a journey through how to still be alert to yourself, your progress and engagement within the virtual workplace, the next chapter will be quick tips and considerations for managing trust, privacy, and your professional and social networks.

CHAPTER 29

TRUST AND PRIVACY

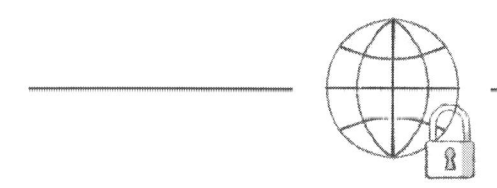

TRUST IN GENERAL IS SUCH A VALUABLE VIRTUE. It takes a very long time to build and can be tarnished in a moment. Trust at work is a topic to spend time looking at in more detail. Trust occurs at many levels. Your company trusts you to do a good job, keep company information confidential and not do anything to put them or yourself at risk. Your teammates trust you to support them to get the job done by doing your part. In meetings, you are trusted to maintain any agreed privacy and to do whatever follow up activities are assigned to you to complete.

Trust can be just seen as a given but I think it is important to spend some time on this area, just to place in your toolkit some wisdom around it. After that, I have tagged on some paragraphs on working with friends and various social networks. Just like the other chapters, take note of the information and refer to it whenever you need to.

Trust at work

In terms of your trust levels at work, be open but don't be foolish. Don't give too much away about yourself at the beginning. Just keep it to the facts – the area you live in, team or company you previously came from and that's it; be mindful of what you are saying. Stories about how you messed up or wild crazy nights out may seem like a great icebreaker but get to know who you are dealing with first as such stories can be damaging to you and only you are responsible for what people know about you.

Privacy

You are the guardian of what the world knows about you. It is so easy to release information, but once it is out, it's out! Speaking is so easy to do. In theory, it's easy to control. The problem is, we often find it harder to consciously control what we want to say and what we don't. Many times, the conversation just flows, drawing you to say more and more. Or you can get that sudden urge to contribute to an ongoing discussion. In your normal lives, how free you choose to be is entirely your choice. In work, I would highly suggest you take more control over what you say, how you share messages and who you speak to.

When joining a new team, you have a very low level of connection and it is time for you to build relationships and your brand. What you say and your initial approach, actually starts working towards what people think about you: your level of maturity, experience and professionalism. The safest approach before you have built relationships is – keep it high level and brief on a personal level and focus on your work, in more detail. You decide what you share.

Decide what you are comfortable with to share professionally. Places you grew up, education, previous companies, hobbies, favourite places to have food. All basic and high level. Some may be happy to also share high level about family structure but that is taking it to another. Only share what you need to share or are comfortable to share. No more than that - your information is a privilege.

When you feel you are at a level of relationship and trust with a colleague, maybe one who has become a friend, then you can decide if you want to have a more in-depth personal conversation with them. Don't overshare and give away valuable information about yourself especially when it isn't someone who has demonstrated that they genuinely want to form a friendship and can be trusted. Just be polite, friendly, and professional always. People don't have the right to have your personal information.

Privacy with work information

Increasingly organisations require information classifications to be applied to your work and emails. These classifications communicate the level of confidentiality and are a guide for how the content should be treated. More broadly, the classification indicates how accessible the information should be. The four main classifications are usually - *Public, Internal, Restricted and Highly Restricted.* You will often have to apply one of these classifications to your work or emails and as a rule to bear in mind, make sure that you do not share any company or client related information outside your organisation unless it is publicly available information or approved for sharing. Let's look at the definitions in a little more depth.

Public – information that has been approved for sharing in public, outside of the organisation. Or information that if shared externally, it would not create a negative impact on the company.

Internal – information that should not be shared outside of the organisation. It is information that is intended to be shared internally only. This classification is usually the default classification for documents created in workplaces is usually shared across the immediate team or internal communications that are shared more broadly from the organisation.

Restricted – information that is sensitive and should only be shared with those who are approved to receive the information. This information should not be shared personally. All customer information has this classification or higher. Sharing such information in an unauthorised way, can lead to having a work disciplinary or being fired for serious misconduct.

Highly restricted – this is information that is highly sensitive. It is the most restricted and cannot be shared widely. If released externally it would be very damaging to the organisation and could put other teams, individuals or customers at risk. Sharing such information in an unauthorised way has the same consequences as above and where the actions are deliberate, there have been criminal charges brought against the perpetrator.

Work produced at work should never be sent to personal email addresses or shared to any unauthorised recipient. Now there are some emails received at work that are public and non-related to work – these are usually related to health and wellbeing: employee vouchers for sociable activities, rota for the gym, etc. If you have colleagues sharing public social information, these are not related to the company, public and would not pose a risk or harm to the organisation. Most organisations have an email monitoring function which will flag emails that should not cross the work to home barrier.

Non-disclosure agreements – these are legally binding agreements not to share any confidential information as defined in the agreement. They are usually signed between two parties or on behalf of companies and can be introduced at the start or end of a time working together. The agreement stops confidential information from being shared with a third party or publicly.

Chatham House rules

Chatham House is an agreement that "the attendees' privacy and what each person said is kept private." This is a term that can be used in some face-to-face meeting settings where sensitive topics will be discussed. The organisers will say, "This meeting is subject to Chatham House rules." This type of verbal agreement is not bulletproof but is a respected code, so be sure to respect the confidentiality of such meetings.

When you are personally in a meeting situation that you want to be kept confidential, before you start divulging anything, request and agree that the conversation is kept confidential. Once you get the verbal signal of agreement, then you can continue the conversation, and hope they keep their word.

I would still say be cautious as far as possible. Don't say anything that would kill you if it was repeated. Sometimes you can get lured into this; people just asking for your opinion on something that happened. Or asking for your thoughts on something that you know is not a topic for discussion. When you do not speak, nobody knows what you are thinking – think before you speak and speak wisely.

> **Wisdom nugget:**
>
> *What you don't say, cannot come back to hurt you. Be careful about the words that come out of your mouth. Also remember, if you are casually bad mouthing someone, the same is likely to happen to you.*

CHAPTER 30

PROFESSIONAL AND SOCIAL NETWORKS

Working with friends

People always caution against working with friends or family and it is for good reason. You are emotionally connected. It is so much harder to maintain the distance needed to be as truly professional and objective as you would be with any non-related colleague. In some organisations' hiring processes, you are even asked to share if you have any family or connections already in the company. If you do have the incidence of a friend joining your team, or you are joining theirs, you will need to be mindful of protecting the friendship. Your sunshiny connection can very quickly turn cloudy as you begin to co-experience the challenges of team dynamics, the competition as spaces higher up reduce and the need to highlight personal achievements arises.

Suddenly your close friend can enter the "can't be trusted" zone if you aren't careful. Be supportive as far as possible and work out a balance to maintain the friendship.

Also, the reality is the situation has changed, and your relationship dynamic will probably have to change too. You become colleagues in the same area. Fighting for survival can drive people to do weird things and change friends into enemies. Beware of the shift in behaviours but don't get emotional. Keep it professional and just understand that levels have changed. Adjust accordingly.

Friendships do not have to end. They can actually flourish in these situations and grow stronger, with an added professional dynamic once work mode and social modes have been agreed and adopted. But if things seem different, like something seems to have changed, check to find out what the reasons are and resolve as far as possible. Just know that sometimes, things do deteriorate, and the friendship weakens. You may not be able to be as open as you possibly once were.

Imagine if you are offered the promotion that your friend also wants in the team. You are soon to become their manager and then it becomes about stepping into the leadership position well, as previously discussed. As in this example, the realities that can occur when working with friends are that you can no longer be as close as you were, or freely discuss your career moves or aspirations - of course, you still work with them and try and retain as much of the original friendship as possible, but just stay *woke* to the new and evolving dynamics of the relationship.

Networking events

Remember, it was a networking event changed my entire career trajectory. External events that are related to your industry are full of potential. You meet so many people, the wider information really opens your eyes and surprisingly beneficial outcomes can develop from a single conversation. There is no need to pretend. Just be professional and the real, authentic *you*- you on your best day. Before entering an event or starting a conversation, shake off anything negative on your mind or that may have happened before. Shift into that version of 'you' on a great day and be open to genuinely connecting.

It took me a while to learn this, as these events can be very daunting at first which can lower your mood, but you have to just shake it off and shift into confidence. Personally, when I actively and positively engaged at networking events, they became very beneficial. I was able to get more perspective on my value, options and even ended up connecting with someone who became my access to an amazing new job. Anything can happen. Focus on forming genuine connections and then follow-up with them.

There can be moments where many events are happening. You don't have to attend them all, feel free to be selective. Assess the topic, speakers and profile of the organisers to decide whether your attendance would be worthwhile. It is important to keep a value on the time used vs value obtained. Use these points below to assess if a networking event will be of value for you to attend:

- Is it an opportunity to meet more senior people in your current area or an area you want to get in to?

- Will it enable you to learn more about your area/industry or the area/industry you want to go into?

- Would it give you the chance to connect with a person or group that you want to meet but don't usually have access to?

Networking events can also be social and still deliver great opportunities too, so you don't have to be limited to professional networking events. And there may also be moments in life when you just want to socialise with other professional people – fine and very acceptable, especially for the many talented single professionals keen to mingle.

> **Wisdom nugget:**
>
> *Keep a list of contacts. After you meet someone new, just make a note of their details, name, company role, where you met and when, and the key things they told you. Follow-up immediately to make sure they have your details too. If you arrange to meet again, just refer to the notes you made and pick up the conversation from where you left off. You will look so organised.*

Protect your well-being and social networks – you need them!

Remember that your family and friends are very important. It is very easy to take them for granted as you get busy with the pressures of work. Be intentional about letting them know that you care. Make a list of people you need to check in with and tick it off. At busy times, a message, or a short call to say "hello" makes a real difference. They are quick gestures that let your loved ones know that though you are busy, you are still thinking of them. A few years into my corporate career, I landed in a situation where I was directly working for a very senior leader, many levels higher than me. She had a high-pressure role and everyone working directly with her was under pressure as a result.

This manager was so driven, so impressive and though working for her was extremely fast paced and demanding, I also viewed it as a great development opportunity. I definitely had an accelerated learning journey, having to think faster and work smarter. The work was very strategic to the business area and I became very committed to my manager's success. To manage the workload, I worked later and later, and over time began to miss events and social gatherings after work. The late-night working slid into needing to work some weekends too. I started missing key family occasions, fun moments, even church. Over time, my focus gradually shifted to just being available at all times to support when required - day, night, during the week or weekend.

Working in this way, I became quite detached from my core person and almost lost myself. I remember one extremely busy period, when to my utter surprise, this manager asked me a non-business related question – how my weekend was. By that time, I had programmed myself to have all her facts at the front of my mind so I was ready whenever she spoke. In no way was I expecting a question about me or my weekend. In the moment, my mind went blank. I even lied, GOD forgive me, just making up an imaginary weekend that I would have previously enjoyed. In reality, I had probably just been working, stressing about things expected for Monday, and trying to squeeze in time with family before catching up on sleep!

Sounds unbelievable but I truly became consumed by work in that role. That was my reality for a season and I include it as a warning to you that it can happen. Especially in the early part of your career, when working with a very senior manager feels so amazing and like a huge privilege. Even if it is a great growth opportunity, it is so important to strike a healthy balance between work and rest. It is critical to carve out time for the things and people outside of work that enhance your life and wellbeing. Managers in demanding roles, dependent on hardworking and reliable people are also unlikely to spot when you are overworked and stressed, so you need to look after yourself. Nobody can do this for you. Set your limits and know when to switch off for rest and recharging – away from your work.

It is true that many jobs will have very pressurised moments, with responsibilities and tasks that really do have major consequences if they are not delivered carefully and to a high standard. So, of course, always take your job seriously; do your best, operate with integrity - doing what you know deep-down is the right thing to do. Always act responsibly. Those things are all important to focus on while at work but bear in mind that you have a life that is bigger than your job. Just keep the *'important but not urgent'* aspects, like a strong family and social network, in your focus and list of priorities. Real time and intention are needed to maintain these valuable support systems.

In the office environment do your work but don't feel you have to be glued to your desk. I spent a long time afraid to get up from my desk as I thought it was looked upon badly. But managers want to see that you are meeting with your customers, colleagues, taking healthy breaks and are interested in what is happening beyond your immediate work. Taking a break or putting a catch-up into your calendar to connect with your colleagues over a beverage is healthy. It is better to develop relationships and friendships in work than to simply be acquainted with your desk.

Remain human. You are working with people, don't get so consumed in work or battle mode that you can't see when someone genuinely needs a coffee break, or to have a chat or just to share a load. It can be so easy to go into self-preservation mode and making sure that you are doing all you need to do to stay ahead, just remember that you are surrounded by many people just like you. The intentional "How are you doing? How is it going?" and listening for a response, shows care and consideration. It doesn't take much to do but can make a big impact.

At the end of the day, it is a job that you will do for a season and work will always need to be done. It is also a time in your life for you to enjoy as far as possible and create a positive impact through your work and contact with colleagues and managers. Be curious about different areas of work and lookout for new opportunities. Continue learning and don't get closed into just one thing, one area or type of work. Getting comfortable can cause you to get stuck in a role and take away years, without you knowing it. A few months can become, a few years and then huge chunks of your life can get consumed. Time you could have used to do those things you dreamt of. Get comfortable with being uncomfortable because you are pushing yourself to achieve more of your potential.

At every stage of your career, keep your personal goals, personal passions, hobbies and side hustles alive. Don't let those things fall away - nurture them even whilst working in your roles. In the next chapter, we will be looking more closely at how you can do this. How you maintain focus on those things that mean the most to you. How you can build on them and remain connected to the vision for your life.

PART EIGHT

STAY TRUE TO YOU

Thrive and flourish

CHAPTER 31

REMAIN CONNECTED TO YOUR VISION

IT'S FUNNY how the energy towards birthdays changes. Early 20's, generally - full on excitement! For the sociable and sentimental types, a big cause for celebration and gifts. There is usually that element of optimism and new possibilities. Then, as the years start adding up, 30's, 40's and beyond, the celebrations tend to adapt... become less flamboyant or extravagant, with the exception, of course, of the ever-committed party animals.

As the rate of change, new discoveries and variety slow down, years get similar as you get older and new birthdays seem to come round more quickly. Again, for those of you keeping life full of spontaneity, surprises, and excitement – I salute you and keep it up! For most of us, however, you can suddenly realise years have rapidly passed by without you being able to account for what you did with them.

I started writing a 'daily' diary entry, to try and keep a more solid record of what was happening each day and where I was in terms of my mindset each day. Commas around daily because I struggled to consistently keep up with writing my diary but having a set time each day before I went to bed helped me to set aside the necessary time to keep it updated. Consistency is the key or you end up with the life gaps, blanks dotted throughout the diary or stretching for weeks or months – I'm guilty of that!

I still have a desire to nail this, as it captures my thoughts, feelings, and approaches to situations in a given season. Looking back over previous years has been a great way to track my personal development and changes. Those who regularly do this will know it's such a valuable way of assessing yourself, who you were and who you are now. It is also very helpful for spotting patterns and things about yourself that you need to work on.

Consistently keeping a daily diary is just a part of staying connected to the vision for your life. Your vision is your desired future position and the ideal picture that you imagine for your life. Your vision brings together who you are as a person, and the dreams and hopes you have for your future and the world around you. Taking some time out to think about it deeply, can really help you get a clearer picture of what it looks like. One of my pastors also refers to your vision as a "divinely inspired picture of your future," so I pray about it from time to time, too.

Writing down your vision takes it out of your mind and brings it into your reality. During your thinking time, you can write down the things that come to your mind about your future and give you peace; what you want to be doing, how you want to be feeling, who you want to be to the world, who you want to have around you. It then becomes something that you can keep as a focal point, to assess if what you are doing and how you are choosing to spend your time, aligns to it. Your vision helps you maintain your perspective through your career and life in general. For those diligent with diary writing, it also helps you to daily look at how close you are getting to it.

Keeping your perspective:

Within your job role, periodically having a personal Micro and Macro review is a good way to keep your perspective on where you are. Usually during your mid-year review is a good moment to have that personal check in with yourself, so let me explain this further:

Micro review – Am I learning new skills? Am I gaining new experiences? Am I in the right team or business area to enable me to develop? Do I enjoy what I am doing? Am I interested in this area?

Macro review – Is the company doing well? Is the business or area strategically important/growing? Are there opportunities for roles at a higher level of seniority and salary that I can move into as I develop my skills and experience?

The micro view is always important but particularly so early on in your career. The macro view can be a consideration from the start as well but really becomes more important when you have developed your 'micro,' as a foundation and desire to locate yourself in the best macro situation to increase your value and earning potential. Having a micro and macro review should also help you align more with the vision you have for your life.

Keeping a *Micro* and *Macro* view of where you are now and how you are developing:

1. You may be in a team or area that is not as strategically important as other areas but gives you the opportunity to learn in an environment with lower demands and pressure. Such a role can give you the time and environment to really learn and develop your level of competence. Your higher skillset then gives you the opportunity to apply for more senior roles in more demanding environments that you are more equipped to take on.

2. You should set a time limit/target for when you want to move to a space or place that offers you more opportunity to develop and is also strategic and growing; use your micro to get you into that new place. This often comes with the macro benefits of higher salary and seniority.

3. There are some opportunities that can arise that are exactly what you need and are of benefit to your development and long-term progression. Sometimes you make find that this ideal role and company offers lower salaries than your current company. Assess what is most important to you in such cases – salary growth or the access to that development opportunity. Weigh up what is best for you. It is also possible that some roles that start as a lower salary may have the potential to grow as passion drives the development of skills.

4. The other thing that happens as you develop your micro-skills and gain experience in macro situations down the

line, is that you may start to spot opportunities to create something that is greatly needed. You may be ready to branch out and start your own business. Assess the risks, make a plan, research what you need to do and any existing ideas, and make contacts. Try it!

Remember, if you are doing a job in one large company, another large company will offer the same or similar job with a potentially higher salary. In the micro season, it is recommended that you switch roles every two to three years. Some people have a great career moving through an organisation. Others move out to other companies and then return, applying for a job at a higher level than when they left. Wherever your journey ends up, don't get dragged along. Always be alert to what is happening around you and the options and the opportunities you have.

Don't tie your life to the vision of an organisation. Whatever company you join, they will have some strategy driving the business. There will be a heap of tasks associated with the overarching business strategy and each one of these strategic initiatives is usually treated as high priority. Just remember this: like politics and governments, the strategy only remains strong as long the initiator is in power or position. When the initiator/visionary moves on or gets fired, the strategy often gets thrown out and replaced by someone else trying to make a name for themselves. When new managers or business leader take over a business area, I have seen years of progress and hard work immediately disregarded, ignored, or totally repackaged and redefined to support the new leadership agenda. Just like that 2, 3, 4 years of hard work completely redirected or replaced.

The reality is that the business plan and goals are not your life plan and goals - don't get that mixed up. I had moments when I was so close to the work that was being delivered by my team and especially where I knew it was highly strategic and had both an internal and external spotlight. I believed that I just needed to pour my whole self into it and that I had the special responsibility and privilege to work on it. This feeling caused me to start working repeated late nights, working over the weekend and ultimately missing key family events and I just had to make regular personal sacrifices to get work done. That is not a healthy balance and does no good for your wellbeing or work in the future. While you are in a job, you help the company achieve its goals and create a positive impact as far as possible but don't neglect those relationships that build your social capital.

Stay focused on *you* – run your own race. We all need to get to the point that we understand what really matters, especially to you. Understand what you want for your life and then have an honest and frank conversation with yourself.

- Money – How much do you need?
- Role direction – Where is your career going?
- Organisation, vision and goals – What type of organisation do you want to work in?
- Your current team – Where are the opportunities for growth?
- Your ability to have a life outside of work – How strong is your social network of family/friends?

Keep what you want for these in focus and make sure you are putting in your work to obtain the best for them. It helps to have conversations with your peers because then you can also benchmark yourself and get more understanding of other people's journey and progress. You should avoid being in competition with others. Be motivated by others but compete with yourself. Commit to pushing for better in your relationships with people, your family, friends, partner/spouse and developing your faith.

Review if the position you are currently working in also works for your life. Can you clearly see the next step? Does it push you closer to your vision? Have you confirmed what you need to do to progress? Have you identified people who can help you? A job should offer you something. It is more than you just working. Again, as mentioned earlier, **time = life**, so the time you spend in a role is how you are spending your life in that season. Your life that is not a rehearsal - this is it, so your years of work need to work for you, your world, the visions you have, and the impact you want to have. Alignment to your life goals and personal vision is key. If you have not defined your personal vision yet, spending time to get clear on the greatest vision for your life and future will be very helpful to you.

Think about how you have already developed. The great things about you, the areas to improve anything negative to leave behind or stop. Think about how you want to be in future and then talk to your mind. Tell your mind who you are in your new state. "I am xxx..., I am xxx...." Start doing different actions in line with this new state. The more you align your action to those achieving that new state the more it becomes your reality! Here is an example of how you could follow a sequence. "I know my stuff, I am xxx, I am an expert, I am xxx...," "I learn, produce and share great results," etc. Take three deep breaths in between each statement. Think about and identify the highest place you want to reach. What opportunities are around you right now? How can you proactively bring those statements to life? Commit to putting the work in, speak to more experienced people for insights to help you develop, focus, even pray about the changes you want to make. Stay *woke* in your work and just go for it.

The moral of the story: don't tie your life to the big strategic goals of your organisation. Contribute to their journey for as long as it makes sense and be ready to let go and move on. The main priority in every job you do is to contribute to the team, while developing skills, experiences and knowledge to keep making you stronger. It is an opportunity to create a network of supporters/references - those who will speak positively about you when you are not even there.

Regularly reflect on the following questions: What is the company/job giving to you? What do you need from the role at the current stage of your life? Then check if you are getting it. If you are, you can choose to remain there or move onto something else. The fact is that no matter how much effort you put into a job, when you leave, someone else will be hired in your place.

Therefore, you are so important. Focus on doing what you need to do, for the right reasons and at the right time. Make decisions that get you closer to your vision of success in life. With that in mind, we now move to looking at one the most common barriers to progress and fulfilment - procrastination. It's so obvious and common but deadly to the attainment of goals and dreams. It so often exists in bad habits and a lack of intentional action to stop it. The reality is, the more you beat your procrastination, the more you live with purpose. The choice is always *yours*.

CHAPTER 32

BEAT PROCRASTINATION AND LIVE WITH PURPOSE

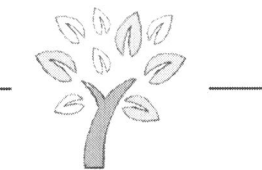

WELCOME TO THE LAST CHAPTER! After all the knowledge shared throughout the book, this final chapter is about refocusing your mind to align with your targets. To look more broadly at what matters and to make sure that you do not allow anything, including yourself, to stand in the way of your progress and highest dreams for your life. We are ending on Procrastination vs Purpose, as a reminder that you need to constantly battle against procrastination and keep moving forward with intention.

Procrastination will come up against the *3 Ps: Progress, Promotion and Pay Rises*. It will also come up against many other areas of your life, too. It is an enemy that you need to defeat personally on the inside. Beating procrastination starts in your mind. Knowing what you need to do and deciding that you are going to do it. Make a commitment to that decision. As discussed in earlier chapters, create a plan for what needs to happen and hold yourself accountable or have others to hold you accountable.

Beware that when you make a decision to smash your goals, your old habits and distractions will try and fight your new commitment. At the point that you decide to focus, you may suddenly start to feel sleepy, or you may suddenly want to eat more, get the urge to get on your phone, etc. Different desires will arise trying to tempt you away from facing your tasks and smashing your goals. Fight those lazy feelings! Accept that you will need to do what you don't feel like doing. It may feel boring or like you are missing out on the enjoyable things, but you are choosing to sacrifice the *now* in order to deliver the potential inside you and enjoy a better future. Whether it is studying to upskill, working towards a professional qualification, preparing for a job interview or completing a personal project, whatever it is; just focus and get it done.

The fact is, your dreams don't become reality now, unless you make the time that you have *now*, count. Move from a place of comfort. For dreams to be achieved, you need to move forward with courage and focus. A great approach I picked up from mentors was: divide your year into quarters. As mentioned in earlier chapters, decide on the goals to be achieved within a set period: three months. Break the 3-month goal(s) into chunks: tasks. Slot all your tasks into a plan and set a deadline to complete each task, as you build towards achieving the overall goal. When you accomplish your goals, it will feel great but keep in mind – your success is never just for you. There is always someone looking up to you, whether you know them or not. When you demonstrate what is possible, it encourages others to dream and aspire.

Questions to ask yourself: What are you supposed to be doing now? What are you capable of? Who could you be in this season of your life? What is in your heart to do? What have you been putting off for too long? Make up your mind to take real action now - **Today**. What tasks need to be completed now? Set deadlines and nail them! Put post-it notes up around your home with your targets to keep you focused. Leave your phone far away from you or decide not to look at it for a few hours. It also helps to tell someone that you are committed to getting it done and ask them to keep you accountable.

Professionally, you can also tell someone whom you respect greatly about your specific deliverables, maybe someone you would be keen to impress. This one is riskier, as your character and integrity are on the line. As you make your commitment more visible, there is increased pressure to do what you said, which should increase your motivation to achieve it. If you deliver what you said, you show integrity, improve your brand and possibly open new doors for yourself. If you fail to do what you said, you may have messed up your whole opportunity with that person. The best approach is to commit to yourself - focus and deliver.

Whenever you are trying to get to that next level and build new muscle, it really hurts but you know it will be worth it. There is a reason you are doing it. There is a *why*. If we come back to the world of work and your career - What is your *why*? What are the reasons that motivate you to keep pushing? These *whys* are the driving force to motivate you to persevere through your work journey, no matter how challenging it may become. It gives you the reason to push past where you are now, towards the progress and benefits you want to see.

Here are a few examples:

- To get a better life for yourself or your family.
- To prove that you are not a statistic or stereotype.
- To break a record or limitations previously set around you.
- To help your loved ones have a better life.
- To get yourself out of debt.
- To be the best you know you can be.
- To maximise the time given to you.
- To prove the doubters wrong.
- To give hope and inspiration to those who look up to you.
- To be able to freely give change to the life of someone who will never be able to thank you.
- To be able to travel without worrying about money.
- To progress even further than your parents.
- To achieve key goals before you get too old.
- To fulfil the purpose you believe you were created for.

It could be none of these, some of these, or maybe just one of these. To be honest, all that matters is that you are clear on your own *whys*. Bring them to the front of your mind and keep them in your focus. Write down what is important to you and stick it on your walls or keep it visible in a notepad. You will need to connect your hope, desires, and faith to what you have written and believe it is possible. Push towards them as goals. The *whys* will give you more energy to put in the work required. I encourage you to stay focused on maximising your potential at work and in every part of your life. Dream big dreams and achieve great goals. To keep up your motivation, be very clear on your reasons and remind yourself of them every day.

Wow, you made it! Congratulations on completing the book! I hope you have already begun to experience the power that comes from waking up to what is available to you personally and professionally. I hope that this book was able to help you see how much more control you can have over your career journey if you are willing to take personal ownership of your actions and apply winning approaches and strategies for progress.

You now own all the insights, approaches and strategies offered to you from my experiences, learning, and workplace observations. To really embed them, keep referring back to the chapters as you need them. As you continue your journey, the main objective is to remain woke as you progress - already being awake. No longer sleeping! You have read this book, so you now have key information and an idea of what's going on around you in the workplace; you have the strategies and so much helpful advice that, if followed, will produce positive results.

Use this book as a solid foundation to help you navigate the workplace and progress with pace. Continue to build even more personal learning and approaches that you, too, can share with those around you. Focus on your personal reasons and go out there and be your extraordinary self! If you do, you will impact the world around you for the better. Proactively manage and drive your career and progression. Let the people who meet you say, "I had the privilege of working with that person." And even if they don't, focus on staying woke and continue to shine!

ACKNOWLEDGEMENTS

To my Omoregie crew – thank you for your great love and creating an amazing home environment for me to flourish and grow. Always cheering me on - you all are an inspiration. Love you.

To my wider family and friends, pastors and mentors, thank you for community and your collective wisdom, encouragement, love and support. To list you all individually would require another book.

In loving memory of Uncle Efosa, Uncle Osaze, Caleb and KD – Your encouragement and love for me was so precious and lives on in my memories. Thank you so much.

Most importantly thanks and glory to GOD who gave me life, talents, and the opportunity to create a positive impact in this world - My Source, guiding me every day and in every situation.

Printed in Great Britain
by Amazon